The Libra Book
Everything You Should Know About Libras

CRAFTED BY SKRIUWER

Copyright © 2025 by Skriuwer.

All rights reserved. No part of this book may be used or reproduced in any form whatsoever without written permission except in the case of brief quotations in critical articles or reviews.

At **Skriuwer**, we're more than just a team—we're a global community of people who love books. In Frisian, "Skriuwer" means "writer," and that's at the heart of what we do: creating and sharing books with readers worldwide. Wherever you are in the world, **Skriuwer** is here to inspire learning.

Frisian is one of the oldest languages in Europe, closely related to English and Dutch, and is spoken by about **500,000 people** in the province of **Friesland** (Fryslân), located in the northern Netherlands. It's the second official language of the Netherlands, but like many minority languages, Frisian faces the challenge of survival in a modern, globalized world.

We're using the money we earn to promote the Frisian language.

For more information, contact : **kontakt@skriuwer.com** (www.skriuwer.com)

TABLE OF CONTENTS

CHAPTER 1: AN INTRODUCTION TO LIBRA
- *Where Libra fits among the zodiac signs*
- *Main qualities linked to balance and fairness*
- *Reasons people find Libra appealing*

CHAPTER 2: LIBRA THROUGH THE AGES
- *Ancient origins and changing views of the constellation*
- *Role of balance in different civilizations*
- *How Libra's meaning evolved over time*

CHAPTER 3: LIBRA'S SYMBOL AND PLANET
- *The scales as a symbol of justice and evenness*
- *Venus's influence on aesthetics and harmony*
- *Connecting the planet's traits to Libra's identity*

CHAPTER 4: THE IDEA OF BALANCE
- *Why balance is central to Libra*
- *Practical ways Libras seek evenness in daily life*
- *Challenges when striving for perfect equilibrium*

CHAPTER 5: NOTABLE PERSONALITY TRAITS
- *Politeness and courtesy in Libra's style*
- *The drive for fairness and peacemaking*
- *Benefits and pitfalls of Libras' characteristic traits*

CHAPTER 6: LIBRA AND FRIENDSHIPS

- *How Libras build strong, balanced bonds*
- *Diplomacy in handling group conflicts*
- *Avoiding over-commitment in social circles*

CHAPTER 7: LIBRA AND ROMANCE

- *Approach to love and partnership*
- *Keeping harmony in emotional connections*
- *Handling disagreements with gentle fairness*

CHAPTER 8: LIBRA AND FAMILY TIES

- *Balancing roles and responsibilities at home*
- *Supporting relatives through calm negotiation*
- *Encouraging open dialogue and kindness*

CHAPTER 9: LIBRA IN THE WORKPLACE

- *Team-oriented approach and leadership style*
- *Diplomacy in office conflicts and negotiations*
- *Finding success by blending courtesy and decisiveness*

CHAPTER 10: DECISION-MAKING AND LIBRA

- *Why Libras weigh multiple sides before acting*
- *Methods to avoid paralysis by analysis*
- *Trusting instincts after gathering facts*

CHAPTER 11: THE EMOTIONAL LIFE OF LIBRA

- *Balancing personal feelings with social harmony*
- *Managing stress and avoiding bottled-up emotions*
- *Empathy and its effect on well-being*

CHAPTER 12: LIBRA AND COMMUNICATION

- *Polite discourse and active listening*
- *Bridging gaps in groups and discussions*
- *Sharing honest truths without harshness*

CHAPTER 13: DAILY ROUTINES FOR LIBRA

- *Creating schedules that support calm and order*
- *Handling chores, hobbies, and work with fairness*
- *Maintaining a peaceful ambiance each day*

CHAPTER 14: MISUNDERSTANDINGS ABOUT LIBRA

- *Common stereotypes and why they are incomplete*
- *Clearing up myths of indecision or superficiality*
- *How Libras show their deeper side*

CHAPTER 15: LIBRA AND PERSONAL INTERESTS

- *Creative hobbies and artistic pursuits*
- *Engaging in community or social-based activities*
- *Balancing multiple interests without overwhelm*

CHAPTER 16: LIBRA AND WELL-BEING

- *Physical and emotional balance for health*
- *Managing stress and setting personal limits*
- *Creating supportive social ties*

CHAPTER 17: LIBRA IN THE ZODIAC PATTERN

- *Libra's place among the twelve signs*
- *Opposite sign Aries and the self-other balance*
- *Seasonal context and cardinal air qualities*

CHAPTER 18: LIBRA'S CONNECTIONS WITH OTHER SIGNS

- *Compatibility highlights for each zodiac sign*
- *Bridging differences through fairness*
- *Tips for building healthy cross-sign relationships*

CHAPTER 19: LIBRA IN DIFFERENT SOCIETIES

- *Global themes of balance and justice*
- *Symbols of scales across cultures and history*
- *Libra's ideals in law, tradition, and social norms*

CHAPTER 20: KEY THOUGHTS ON LIBRA

- *Recap of Libra's central ideas and values*
- *Applying Libra's lessons to everyday life*
- *Why balance remains an ongoing pursui*

CHAPTER 1: AN INTRODUCTION TO LIBRA

Libra is one of the twelve zodiac signs that many people talk about when they look at the stars and try to learn about personality traits or ways of thinking. People often say that Libra is all about balance and harmony. This sign is usually linked to a time of year that begins around the end of September and goes until near the end of October. Many folks believe that people born under Libra have a special way of seeing fairness in everyday life. They might enjoy peace and calm, and they might look for ways to get along with everyone around them.

When people speak about zodiac signs, they sometimes imagine the sky as a big circle cut into twelve parts. Each part lines up with one of the signs, such as Aries, Taurus, Gemini, Cancer, Leo, Virgo, Libra, Scorpio, Sagittarius, Capricorn, Aquarius, and Pisces. The idea is that these signs may hint at certain personality traits or patterns. While not everyone believes the zodiac affects life events, many find it interesting to read about these signs and notice if any traits seem to match the way they act or feel.

Libra is the seventh sign in the zodiac group. It comes after Virgo and before Scorpio. Some people think it is special because it sits in the middle of the cycle, which stretches from early in the year (Aries in late March) to the end of winter (Pisces in late February). Since Libra is in the middle of the zodiac, some say it serves as a bridge. It might show the shift between different parts of the year. In many parts of the world, late September to late October is when summer is ending and fall is picking up. This can be a season of change in weather, with temperatures going down and leaves changing color.

Some link Libra's sense of balance to this time, because the days and nights around the start of Libra can be close to equal lengths in some places.

Even though each zodiac sign is said to have a different focus, Libra stands out for its link to balance in many areas. For instance, Libras may look for fairness in arguments. They might want to make sure everyone gets along and that problems are worked out in a calm way. This does not mean Libra people never get upset or never fight. But it does mean they might try hard to keep things peaceful when they can. If two friends are in a quarrel, a Libra might try to help them talk it out so they can find a middle ground.

A common idea is that Libra is an air sign. In astrology, the twelve signs are split into four groups of three signs each. The four groups are often connected to the four elements: fire, earth, air, and water. Aries, Leo, and Sagittarius are fire signs; Taurus, Virgo, and Capricorn are earth signs; Gemini, Libra, and Aquarius are air signs; and Cancer, Scorpio, and Pisces are water signs. The air element is sometimes linked with thoughts, communication, and ideas. That suggests Libras might be quite social or friendly. They could be good at talking with others, sharing new thoughts, or learning fresh things from friends and family.

Some folks say that because Libra is an air sign, it brings a light and breezy mood to relationships. That might mean a Libra will try to stay cheerful and kind with others. They might like to have a good conversation, hear different ideas, and make sure no one is left out. Of course, real life can be complex, and not every Libra person is exactly like this. But people who study star signs often point to Libra when they want to show an example of a balanced thinker who wants to be fair.

Balance is a big word that comes up when talking about Libra. In everyday life, balance can mean many things. It can mean having the right amount of time for school, work, rest, and play. It can mean having the right amount of quiet time and group time. It can also mean treating people with equal respect. Someone who is known as balanced might try to see both sides of an issue before making a choice. Some Libra folks might feel happy when all parts of their life are in a calm place. If something is out of place, they might feel uneasy. They might keep working until things seem even and fair again.

Another idea linked to Libra is harmony. Harmony can mean a pleasing or peaceful arrangement of parts, like notes in music or people in a group. A Libra might do well when things seem calm and in order. They could get uncomfortable if there is a lot of chaos or loud tension between people. Because of this, some people say Libras are good peacemakers. They might try to settle fights or calm heated discussions. This is not to say Libras will always do that well, but it can be a natural thought for many who read about Libra traits.

While it can seem nice to be fair and balanced all the time, there are also times when Libras may struggle. If someone tries to make everything even and perfect, they might end up feeling stuck. They might have trouble choosing which side to take or what action to do, because they want to do the most fair thing. As a result, some people say Libras are sometimes slow to make decisions, or they change their minds if they think they might have made a choice that is not the best for everyone.

In this first chapter, we want to give a wide view of what Libra is about, without going too deep into specific topics like the Libra symbol or the planet that connects to Libra. We will look at those details later. For now, think of Libra as a sign that many people link with justice, fairness, balance, and peace. If you have a friend or classmate who was born during Libra time, you may notice they sometimes show these traits. You might see them step in to fix problems among friends, or they might try to keep things relaxed and friendly.

In fact, for many young people, reading about Libra can be a way to think about how we treat each other. Do we care about fairness? Do we think it is important to be polite and listen to what others have to say? Libra might encourage us to find calm solutions to problems. Instead of letting an argument get worse, maybe we can talk it out. Instead of ignoring someone's ideas, maybe we can listen and give feedback. In this sense, Libra's focus on harmony can be a useful reminder in daily life, no matter what your star sign might be.

Another interesting thing to know is that Libras often like to share. They might enjoy sharing a snack or a game with a friend. This can come from their desire to keep everyone pleased and included. They may think life is better when people are treated equally. This might not always mean they are pushovers or that they let others do whatever they want. Many Libras have firm ideas about right and wrong. But they try to express these ideas in a way that is gentle and polite if they can. They may want to avoid major conflicts, so they prefer talking things through.

People sometimes ask, "If Libra is all about balance, does that mean someone with a Libra birthday never has problems?" Of course not. Everyone faces problems, no matter their birthday. But a Libra might handle problems by searching for the middle path. If they have a group project at school, and friends are arguing over how to do it, a Libra might say, "Let's find a way to mix everyone's suggestions," or "Let's take a vote so we can be sure everyone feels good about the choice." These are typical ways that a Libra might keep the group together.

Some people think Libra has a connection to art and beauty. They say that Libra types like things to look nice, neat, and balanced. They might like arranging their room in a certain way or wearing clothes that match in color. This is sometimes explained by the idea that Libra is ruled by a planet that represents love and beauty. But we will talk more about that planet later in a separate chapter. For now, it is enough to say that Libras can enjoy things that look or sound pleasing. They may be drawn to music, painting, or other forms of expression that bring out harmony.

When you think about Libra, you might also think about the importance of friendship. Libras can be social, though this does not mean they are always outgoing or loud. They might enjoy being around people, but in a gentle way. They might have a few close friends or they might have a big circle of friends they connect with. Either way, Libras can be good listeners who like to offer support. In times of conflict, they can be the ones to calm things down with a kind word or a well-timed suggestion to rest and talk later.

You can also note that Libras may be quite clever in debates. Because they like fairness, they might look at both sides of an issue before they speak. This can help them build logical arguments. They might try to find the strengths in each side, which can be useful if they want to come up with a fair solution. However, the flip side to this is that Libras can get stuck if they see too many sides to a problem. They might feel it is hard to pick one choice. So, they can go back and forth if they think both sides have a good reason. This is something people sometimes call "indecisiveness."

Though this sign focuses on harmony, that does not mean Libras never disagree with anyone. They can still have strong beliefs. But they might try to express them kindly. For example, if a Libra sees someone being unkind, they might speak up, but they will likely do so in a firm, calm way. They might explain how the person's actions are affecting others, hoping the person will understand and change. This is different from some signs that may raise their voice right away. A Libra can try to find a more peaceful approach.

Many people find Libras to be friendly, diplomatic, and charming. This can help them make new friends easily. They might not always share their deeper feelings right away, but they can make conversation that keeps people interested. They might enjoy telling jokes, discussing a variety of topics, and asking others for opinions. Because they want everyone to feel included, they might be good at bringing shy people into the conversation. You might see this in a classroom setting, where a Libra tries to make sure no one is left behind.

There is also a playful side to many Libras. Since they like peace, they might enjoy fun group activities that bring people together. This can include sports, games, or group projects. They might be the type to say, "Let's all do something we can enjoy at the same time." They do this because they like the thought of many people sharing a good time without conflict or arguments. However, when something does go wrong, a Libra may act as the peacemaker once again, trying to fix the situation in a friendly manner.

We should also note that not everyone born under Libra will act the same way. There are many things that shape a person's character: family, friends, culture, experiences, and more. Astrology is just one way people have tried to guess personality traits for a very long time. Some folks find it fun and see some parts of themselves in the sign's descriptions. Others might say it does not match them at all. That is okay. Nobody has to believe the same things. The interesting thing about Libra, though, is that it is a sign that highlights the concept of balance. Many cultures have shown respect for the idea that everything works better when things are balanced. So even if someone does not follow zodiac signs, they might still think it is good to keep fairness in mind.

To keep from getting confused, it can help to remember that each zodiac sign has its own themes. Libra's main theme is fairness and harmony. If you see someone who is always trying to do what is fair for everyone, or who talks a lot about what is right, you might guess they are a Libra. Or if not, they might just share some traits that people often link to Libra. But if they are actually a Virgo or Scorpio, that is fine too. Humans are more complex than just one label.

For a child reading about Libra, the idea of fairness can be an important lesson. Fairness is something we learn about early in life, like when we share toys or snacks, or when we let everyone have a turn playing a fun game. Libra can remind us that it is good to think about how our choices affect others. It also shows us that being peaceful can help solve problems. Of course, we cannot always avoid disagreements, but Libras might try to handle them in a calm way. This may involve talking, listening, and finding solutions that help everyone feel better.

In this book, we will discuss many aspects of Libra. We will look at how Libra has been viewed in the past, what people think about Libra's symbol, and how Libras might deal with friendships, love, and other parts of life. Each chapter will focus on a different topic so that we can see how Libra's ideas about balance and fairness might show up in many situations. By the end, you should have a much clearer picture of what Libra stands for, how people talk about it, and how you might spot these traits in yourself or others.

We will keep things simple and avoid using tough words. The main idea to know right now is that Libra is a star sign often linked to fairness, kindness, and calm. It is an air sign, which often points to a mind that likes ideas and communication. People born under this sign may want to keep things peaceful, make choices that are fair, and think carefully about different sides of a problem. While no one is perfect, and every person is unique, Libra's themes can be a good reminder that peace and fairness are often worth seeking.

As you read further, you might think about how balance appears in your everyday life. Do you try to balance how much time you spend studying with how much time you spend relaxing or playing? Do you try to be fair to friends or classmates who might not have the same opinion as you? Do you notice when things feel uneven or unfair? These kinds of thoughts can help you connect with Libra's focus on harmony.

This introduction should give you a solid understanding of the basics of Libra. Now that we have some background, we can look at how Libra has appeared across different points in history. We will see how various groups of people viewed Libra or how they saw the concept of balance as an important force in life. That is what we will explore in the next chapter. By doing so, we can better grasp why Libra remains a sign that many people find appealing and worth talking about.

CHAPTER 2: LIBRA THROUGH THE AGES

In this chapter, we will talk about how the idea of Libra, or the concept of balance, has been understood in different periods and in different parts of the world. While the modern zodiac is often connected to certain months and traits, people have looked at the stars for a long time. Many ancient peoples had their own ways of naming star groups, and they often gave them meanings or stories. Libra was no exception. Though various cultures described the stars differently, the concept of a balanced scale has shown up in more than one place throughout history.

Long ago, in Mesopotamia (a region where some of the earliest civilizations began), the night sky was very important. The people there watched the stars to know when to plant crops and to keep track of seasons. They created one of the oldest known systems of constellations. Some say that Libra used to be part of the constellation of Scorpio. The stars that now make up Libra might have been seen as the claws of the Scorpion by some groups. Later on, this same group of stars took on the image of scales, which fit the idea of balance. This change might have happened because people noticed that the sun passed through these stars at a time when day and night were roughly equal in length. They linked this to fairness or equality.

In ancient Babylonian astronomy, the scales might have also been connected to a specific god who represented law and justice. The idea of justice lines up well with the symbol of scales. Think of a scale: it has two pans and tries to weigh things so that both sides are level. That is a clear symbol of fairness. This shape was later carried on into Greek and Roman traditions. The Babylonians were skilled observers of the sky, and they left records that helped shape later astrological systems.

Moving on, ancient Egypt had many important symbols that revolved around balance and judgment. For example, they had the concept of weighing the heart against a feather in the afterlife. Though this does not directly refer to Libra, you can see how the idea of scales and fairness was important. Some scholars suggest that the Egyptian concept of balance might have influenced how Greek and Roman thinkers viewed the stars. When Greece and Rome grew in power, they adopted many ideas from older civilizations, including the idea of dividing the sky into twelve parts.

During the time of ancient Greece, people like Ptolemy studied and wrote about the zodiac. The Greeks believed that each sign had certain traits. Libra, linked to the scales, was often talked about in the context of justice and fairness. In Greek myths, there are stories about gods who weigh the lives or actions of humans, showing that justice was a valued concept. The sign of Libra, as a pair of scales, fit nicely into this mindset. The Greeks gave each sign a name that reflected a certain figure or object. For Libra, they chose the idea of the scales, which can also be called "the balance."

The Romans, who admired much of Greek culture, carried on this star lore. They used similar names for the constellations. Latin words became the basis for many of these signs. The Latin word "libra" can mean scales or a balance. It also referred to a unit of weight. This is where the English abbreviation "lb" for pound in weight partly comes from. In Roman society, fairness was a theme in law and civic life. They built courts and had laws that they believed should apply to all Roman citizens. So the symbol of Libra fit into their sense of justice. Over time, as Rome became the main power in the region, the zodiac as we know it spread throughout the empire.

Jumping forward, the idea of Libra and its link to fairness did not vanish with the fall of Rome. In the medieval and Renaissance periods in Europe, astrology continued to be studied by scholars, including doctors and astronomers. They believed that the positions of the stars could influence a person's health, personality, and even events on Earth. Libra was still the sign that stood for balance. Many illustrated manuscripts from those times show the zodiac wheel, with Libra drawn as a set of scales. These manuscripts might have decorated pages with detailed artwork to show each sign. Libra usually appears as a person holding scales or just the scales by themselves.

Throughout these periods, the overall meaning of Libra stayed much the same: it represented the theme of fairness. People who looked to the stars believed that those born under Libra would display balance in how they interacted with others. Some medieval texts also said Libras would be calm, friendly, and helpful. Of course, these were broad ideas, and not every text agreed. But the scales were always there as the main symbol, reminding readers that this sign is connected with equality and harmony.

As time went on, astrology became more common in some cultures and less common in others. In certain places, people studied it seriously and wrote long books about how star signs might affect people's futures. In other places, it was seen only as a passing interest or even dismissed. But the image of Libra as the scales remained. In modern times, you can open a newspaper or a website and see a horoscope for Libra. That horoscope might talk about the day's focus on fairness or mention how the sign's desire for peace might help with relationships.

When we think about Libra through the ages, we can see it has a link to the idea of balance that runs across many cultures. Although not every culture named these stars "Libra," many had a concept of scales or balance as important. This repeats in stories about gods who weigh good and evil, or about laws that treat people equally. It shows that humans everywhere tend to value fairness in some shape or form.

In some Eastern traditions, zodiac systems developed differently than in the West. For instance, the Chinese zodiac uses animals for each year, not month. That system does not focus on Libra the way Western astrology does. But that does not mean the idea of balance was missing. Many Eastern philosophies also talked about harmony in different ways. For example, the concept of yin and yang in Chinese thought is about two forces that need to remain in balance to keep the world in order. Though it is not about the Libra symbol, it does show how widely the theme of balance appears.

In modern popular culture, Libra can be found in many forms. You might see references to Libra in books, television, or online articles. People who follow astrology closely may wear jewelry with the Libra sign or keep a small scale figure as a reminder of fairness. Some individuals like to point out that Libra time of year often includes changes in the season, which might remind us that nature has its own form of balance between hot and cold, or day and night. It is interesting how one set of stars in the sky, interpreted thousands of years ago, is still part of what people read about in horoscopes today.

You might wonder why so many cultures kept the idea of Libra or adopted it once they learned it. One reason could be that scales as a tool are easy to understand. They measure weight evenly, and they help traders and customers check if a deal is fair. Even if some societies did not picture those particular stars as scales at first, the symbol of a balanced scale was too fitting to ignore. It matched the time of year when day and night felt balanced, at least in places where the equinox was noticeable. Because the sign lined up with that period, it made sense to keep or adapt the idea of the scales.

Today, some people do not pay much attention to astrology, while others read about it every day. Either way, many still talk about Libra as a symbol of fairness. Even if someone does not believe in zodiac predictions, the shape of the scales can be a neat reminder of how important it is to treat others equally. You might see Lady Justice in modern law buildings, holding scales to show the same principle: everyone should get fair treatment. Libra and Lady Justice are not the same, but they share the concept of balanced scales as a guide for how things should be in an ideal world.

Learning about Libra through the ages also teaches us that ideas can travel across different lands. Whether it was Mesopotamia, ancient Greece, Rome, medieval Europe, or modern society, the sign of Libra kept appearing. People might change small details, but the main theme stayed strong. This is partly because the actual stars in the sky remain the same, but also because the idea of fairness does not go out of style. It is something that many people hope to see in their communities and in their own lives.

We can also note that astrologers who lived centuries ago often used simpler tools compared to what we have now. They had to watch the sky closely, make sketches, and follow the motion of stars over time. With all that effort, they formed systems that influenced how people thought about personality and fate. Over time, these astrological ideas spread through trade routes and conquests. The Roman Empire, for example, was big and covered many regions, helping spread Roman ideas, including the zodiac. After the empire's decline, smaller kingdoms and the medieval Church kept or adapted some of these ideas. Libraries held manuscripts with star charts and explanations of each sign, which scholars might copy and share.

During the Renaissance, interest in Greek and Roman knowledge became strong again, leading to new writings about astrology. People then combined these older texts with their own observations to refine or expand on zodiac lore. By this point, Libra was a standard part of the twelve-sign wheel in Europe. Later on, as European nations sailed across the world, they carried these zodiac ideas even further. That is how we find references to Libra in many places today, even those far from the Middle East or Europe.

It is also worth mentioning that during certain periods, astrology was studied by some of the best mathematicians and astronomers of the time, because it was closely tied to astronomy. In order to cast accurate horoscopes, they had to calculate the positions of planets and stars. This led to improvements in math and the creation of more detailed star charts. Even though many modern scientists do not consider astrology a science, we can see that historically, astrology pushed people to observe and measure the skies in systematic ways. Libra was a piece of that puzzle: plotting when the sun would enter Libra, how long it would stay there, and how that timing lined up with the autumn season.

Across these changes, Libra stayed tied to the idea of balance. It is an example of how one symbol can carry meaning from ancient times all the way to modern days. By learning how Libra was viewed in these different periods, we can see how people have consistently valued fairness. Although the exact stories and beliefs have changed, the concept of a balanced scale to show justice remains the same.

In summary, Libra's story began in the ancient world, where the stars that now form the Libra constellation might have been seen as part of Scorpio's claws. Over time, they became known as the scales, especially during the Babylonian and later Greek and Roman periods.

The link to fairness and justice stayed strong because of how well it matched the idea of day and night balancing around the time of the autumn equinox. This theme stayed alive through medieval Europe, the Renaissance, and into modern times. People used Libra as a reminder that balance is valuable, both in the laws of the land and in personal life. Even in places where Western astrology was not the main system, the idea of balance existed in other forms, showing how universal this concept can be.

Now that we have looked at Libra's roots across different ages, we can see why it is often labeled as the sign of fairness and harmony. In the next chapters, we will explore Libra's symbol and the planet many believe is linked to Libra. Then we will look at Libra's main themes and how they might appear in different parts of life, like friendships and work. This historical background helps show why Libra still holds such a strong place in discussions about personality and the zodiac. It has come a long way, but it continues to stand for fairness in the eyes of many who follow these ideas.

CHAPTER 3: LIBRA'S SYMBOL AND PLANET

The symbol most often linked to Libra is a pair of scales. You might picture a balance tool you see in old drawings, where two small dishes hang from a horizontal bar. In everyday life, scales can measure the weight of items. For Libra, the idea of balance applies not only to physical weight but also to fairness. When people see Libra's symbol, they often think about trying to treat everyone in an equal way. This focus on equality can be a core trait for many people who read about Libra.

In astrology drawings, Libra's scales are usually shown level, not tipping to one side. This is a simple way of showing that Libra's main theme is evenness. If something tilts the scales, it can mean that something is unfair or out of order. People say that when a Libra notices imbalance, they might feel the need to fix it. This might appear in everyday situations, such as splitting time fairly or sharing things with friends. The scales are a quick reminder that Libra often cares about keeping things steady.

Long ago, these same stars in the sky were sometimes seen as the claws of Scorpio, but over time, people came to view them as a separate group forming the shape of a scale. That shape caught on because it fit with the time of year when Libra's period happens. Some people point to the fact that around the start of Libra season, day and night can be close to equal length in some regions. This helped people link the scales with an equal balance of light and dark, which supports Libra's theme of fairness.

Scales also appear in other parts of life, like in law and in old markets. In many courthouse statues, you might see a figure holding scales. This is often a symbol of justice, reminding everyone that laws should be applied fairly. Similarly, in some paintings of old markets, traders used simple hanging scales to weigh goods. These images of scales in different areas of society show how a single object can represent a bigger idea. For Libra, that idea is about seeking fairness.

Moving to the next part of Libra's identity, we come to its ruling planet. In modern Western astrology, people often say Libra is guided by the planet Venus. Venus is sometimes thought of as the planet of love, beauty, and delight. In old stories, Venus (or Aphrodite in Greek myths) stood for kindness, art, and attraction. Many believe that a sign ruled by Venus might show these traits in various ways. For Libra, this might include a fondness for pretty things, nice sounds, or calm settings. It can also mean looking for warmth in relationships.

Venus is known in the sky as both the morning star and the evening star at different times. It can be one of the brightest objects seen from Earth, which made it important to people long ago. They told many stories about this bright planet. When linked to Libra, Venus is said to bring an extra focus on harmony. Some folks say Libras might like to see beauty in their surroundings. They might enjoy arranging their rooms in a neat way or picking colors that go well together.

However, not every Libra person will be an artist or lover of fancy clothes. The link to Venus is more of a suggestion that Libra types can be drawn to gentle and pleasant things. It might mean they prefer friendly conversation over arguments. It could mean they notice when someone is feeling left out and try to bring them into the group. In many ways, Venus is thought to add softness to Libra's idea of fairness, leading to a sign that wants to bring people together in a kind way.

Some people say that Venus also stands for relationships of all sorts, not only romantic ones. Because Libra is ruled by Venus, many believe this sign values friendships, teamwork, and close bonds. Libras might see their friends as special people who deserve respect and support. The desire for fairness can show up in these relationships, such as when a Libra tries to share time equally among different friends or tries to keep arguments from getting too harsh. The presence of Venus may make them more aware of how everyone is feeling.

The scales and Venus together form a picture of how Libra might act. The scales alone stand for the pursuit of justice and the quest for balance. Venus adds the touch of warmth that encourages calm rather than roughness. This does not mean Libras never get angry or upset, but they might try to settle conflicts in a softer way. They might also show a desire to listen to others and look for a fair path that respects everyone involved.

Some astrological thinkers compare Libra's use of scales to a person weighing different ideas in their mind. The mind is always trying to measure and balance opposing thoughts or feelings. When the planet Venus influences these scales, it can mean that the decision-making process often includes concern for how choices will affect relationships or the pleasantness of a situation. A Libra might think: "If I do this, will everyone be comfortable? Will it be good for the overall harmony of the group?" This can be a strong guiding force in their actions.

People who read horoscopes might notice that the planet connected to a sign can be mentioned in daily predictions. For example, an astrologer might write, "Venus is moving in a way that helps Libras find more comfort in their home life." This is a common way to blend the idea of Libra, the concept of balance, and Venus's themes of comfort and beauty. Whether or not these predictions come true, many readers enjoy keeping an eye on how the planet's position might match their experiences.

The symbol for Venus itself is a circle with a small cross beneath it. You may have seen it used to represent the female gender in biology or on signs for women's restrooms. In astrology, that symbol also stands for the planet that rules Taurus and Libra. People who study star signs sometimes say that while Taurus might show the earthy, practical side of Venus (like a love of physical comfort), Libra might show the airy, social side of Venus (like a desire for companionship and fairness).

Another point to keep in mind is that Libra is often described as a masculine sign, even though it is ruled by a feminine planet. In astrology, "masculine" and "feminine" are old ways of grouping signs, not necessarily about actual gender. Masculine signs are said to be more outward or active, while feminine signs are more inward. Libra is an air sign, and air is often described as active and intellectual. So, you have a blend of the airy, active quality of Libra with the softer, more caring energy of Venus. Many people say this blend can result in a pleasant, friendly nature.

The scales themselves have a more neutral feel, neither clearly masculine nor feminine. They just show a tool that weighs items. But the planet that leads Libra's outlook might bring an extra layer of warmth and kindness. This can be seen in how Libras might enjoy social events, small gatherings, or peaceful outings. They might look for ways to beautify their environment or to show kindness to those around them.

Some who look at astrology also connect Libra's symbol to the letter Omega (Ω) in the Greek alphabet, or say it looks like a horizon with the sun rising above it. These are just visual comparisons. The typical meaning stays the same: a balanced scale. It is interesting that this shape, which might have begun as a small design, is now recognized around the world as Libra's sign. It shows that even a simple image can hold a bigger idea that lasts through time.

If you meet someone who is strongly connected to Libra, they might enjoy talking about how the scales reflect their sense of justice. They could also mention how they feel drawn to nice things or how they love bringing smiles to people's faces. They might believe that Libra's ruling planet helps them focus on kindness. Of course, real personalities can vary a lot, and star signs are just one way to think about them. Still, many find it fun to match up these traits with the sign's symbol and planet.

In some older astrological texts, each planet was said to have a special day of the week, color, or type of metal linked to it. Venus, for instance, was sometimes tied to the color green or pink, and linked to copper as a metal. While these connections may not be as well-known in modern times, people who enjoy these links might wear copper jewelry or choose gentle colors because it makes them think of Libra and Venus. It can be a personal way to feel closer to the sign's spirit.

Libra's symbol can also be found in art and products. For example, someone might design a necklace or a piece of home décor showing the balanced scales. Others might design items using the planet Venus's symbol. Some people like these visuals because they remind them of fairness, friendship, or calm living. They see the sign's artwork as a hint to keep things balanced. This is one way that astrology seeps into everyday life, even for those who do not read horoscopes often.

Another thing you might hear is that Libra, being guided by Venus, may enjoy what is sometimes called "the good life." That could mean they like tasty food, pleasant music, or a quiet setting that feels welcoming. Since the scales also remind them not to go overboard, they might try not to indulge too much. However, some Libras might still struggle with choices, like picking what dessert to eat. They might weigh different options because they want to find the most pleasing choice without ignoring what others want.

Together, the scales and Venus create an image of a sign that seeks balance in both mind and heart. The scales encourage Libra to be objective, to check both sides, and to treat people fairly. Venus brings a caring or gentle side, reminding Libra to keep relationships happy. This mix can lead to a personality that tries to please friends and family, while also being thoughtful about what is right or wrong. Some people find that Libras can smooth rough waters, although they might also get stuck if they cannot decide quickly.

Many times, people focus on Libra's social nature, suggesting that Libras might do well in group activities. That also ties back to Venus's idea of bonding with others. A Libra may prefer not to work alone for too long. They could feel more energized when in a team, especially if they have a say in keeping things fair for everyone. The scales stand for the checks and balances they apply to group tasks, and the planet of love and beauty might boost their desire to create a pleasing atmosphere.

If you are looking to understand why Libras might have a gentle style of communication, remember that the planet that rules them is often linked to the idea of peace and calm. This can shape how a Libra reacts when things get heated. They might try to remain composed, speak kindly, and find a middle ground. Meanwhile, the scales keep them from ignoring logic. They do not simply follow emotions; they try to reason with facts and fairness. Of course, this is the ideal version. Real people vary in how they handle conflicts.

The image of Libra's scales also shows up in star maps. If you use a star chart app during the time of the year when the sun is in Libra, you can see where the constellation lines are drawn. It may not look exactly like a perfect set of scales in the sky, but once you connect the dots, you can see the shape people used to label as Libra. This can be a fun activity if you want to see how ancient observers assigned shapes to the stars. You can think about how the planet Venus might appear near or within that region at certain times.

An interesting fact: in old Roman units, "libra" meant a pound in weight. That is why the abbreviation for pound is "lb." This is another way we can see the idea of weighing or balancing continuing through language. Though not everyone notices the link, it is still there. It shows how strong the concept of the scale was in ancient daily life. They used it so often in commerce that the word "libra" became a common term for weight.

In summary, Libra's symbol is the scale, and its ruling planet is Venus. The scale reminds people of justice, equal measure, and the wish to see things in balance. Venus brings warmth, friendliness, and an eye for beauty. Libras might try to mix both ideas in their day-to-day life. They could look for solutions that are both fair and kind. Even if you are not a Libra or do not believe in astrology, the image of scales can still be a helpful reminder to treat others equally, and the idea of Venus can serve as a reminder to care for others along the way.

CHAPTER 4: THE IDEA OF BALANCE

Balance is a key concept that shows up in many cultures, and it is very important when talking about Libra. To balance something means you arrange different parts so that no side is too strong or too weak. In daily life, balance can mean giving the right amount of attention to different tasks, like schoolwork, chores, time with friends, and rest. When people think of Libra, they often picture someone who tries to manage all these areas without letting one take over everything else.

For example, if you imagine a seesaw on a playground, it works best when the weight on both ends is roughly equal. If one side is much heavier, that side stays down on the ground while the other side is up in the air. In a similar way, a person might think of their life as needing balance between serious work and fun. If they do too much work, they might feel worn out. If they only play, they might fall behind on important tasks. Libra is a sign that reminds us to keep these parts of life in check.

Balance can also apply to how we use our energy. Sometimes, a person might feel excited in the morning, but as the day goes on, their energy drops. If they push too hard without rest, they might burn out. Libra's focus on balance suggests that taking breaks can help us stay calm and do our best. This does not mean we avoid hard work. It means we try to find a steady pace that keeps us healthy and in good spirits.

When people say Libras look for balance, they might mean more than just time or chores. They could also be talking about emotions. Sometimes, a person can have big feelings, whether they are happy, upset, or worried. If those feelings get overwhelming, it might be hard to think clearly. Libra's sense of balance can mean trying to keep these feelings in a comfortable range. That does not mean ignoring emotions. It simply means letting yourself feel them but also finding a way to calm down and see different sides of a situation.

Another angle of balance for Libra is the idea of fairness among people. In groups, some individuals might speak loudly while others stay quiet. A Libra person may try to invite everyone to share their thoughts, so nobody is left out. This might happen in a classroom discussion or in a family talk. By keeping an eye on who has or has not talked, Libras can help keep the group balanced. This not only prevents conflict but can also show respect for everyone's ideas.

Balance in friendships can mean making sure you treat your friends with kindness and attention, but also giving them space to do their own thing. A Libra might want to see that each friend feels valued. If one friend starts to overshadow the group or always decides what everyone does, the Libra might say, "Let's also hear what someone else wants." This can keep the group from leaning too much in one direction. Of course, this depends on each individual's approach, but Libra as a sign often points to this kind of behavior.

Balance can also apply to how you think about different opinions. Suppose you have a group project and half the group wants to do it one way, while the other half wants another way. A Libra might suggest looking at the pros and cons of each choice. By weighing these points carefully, the group can see if there is a middle approach that takes good ideas from both sides. This does not always work perfectly, but it can be a sign's way of finding harmony.

In some traditions, balance is seen as a strong value. For instance, in certain philosophies, people say that extremes can cause problems. By staying in the middle path, you avoid the dangers of being too rigid or too careless. This idea fits well with Libra's symbol of the scales, which always aim for a level position. Libras can try to stay away from going to extremes in thoughts or actions, though they are not always perfect at it. It is a goal they often think about.

However, there can be challenges to seeking balance all the time. Someone who tries to keep everything perfectly even might struggle when they have to pick sides or act fast. They may worry about upsetting the balance or leaving out someone's view. This can lead to indecision. A Libra might take extra time to think through different angles, which can frustrate people who want quick action. So, while balance can be helpful, it can also cause delays when a clear-cut decision is needed.

Another area of life where balance appears is in taking care of yourself. Many people try to fit exercise, healthy meals, sleep, and hobbies into a busy schedule. A Libra person might be good at noticing if they are focusing too much on one area while ignoring another. For example, if they have been studying a lot, they might realize they need some rest or time with friends. If they have been relaxing too much, they might push themselves to finish their tasks. This sense of moderation can help them stay on track.

Balance can also shape how Libras interact in romantic relationships. They might want both people to have equal voice in decisions. They could try to share tasks and responsibilities so that one person does not feel burdened. Of course, this does not always happen perfectly, but it is often a goal. If disagreements occur, a Libra might step back and ask questions to understand each person's side before finding a middle ground. This approach can keep the relationship stable, as long as each person is willing to talk things out.

Some individuals argue that this focus on balance can make Libras appear unsure at times. Because they see good points on both sides, they might say, "I can see why you think that," followed by, "But I can also see this other point." This can make them sound like they cannot decide. In reality, they might just want to ensure they make the fairest choice. This can be both a strength and a weakness, depending on the situation. When a fast decision is not required, it can help them gather all the facts. When urgency is needed, it can feel like they are stalling.

There is also an idea that balance applies to how Libra sees beauty. This might mean liking colors that go well together or arranging furniture in a way that feels pleasing. If something looks lopsided, a Libra might fix it to make it look more balanced. This does not mean all Libras are interior designers, but many could be extra aware of how things fit together visually. They might notice if a picture on the wall is crooked or if the colors in a painting clash. This small detail can also be a reflection of their desire for harmony in surroundings.

Beyond appearances, some people connect balance to the deeper sense of well-being. If the environment around a person feels chaotic or messy, it might stress them. For a Libra, fixing clutter or adding a small decoration can bring calm. This is part of keeping balance in one's environment. It does not have to be fancy, just tidy enough to create a sense of order. Some Libras feel uneasy when they see a lot of disarray, so they try to arrange things in a neat way.

We can also talk about balance in a community sense. A Libra might want to make sure that rules are fair for everyone. They could get involved in discussions about fairness at school or in local groups. For instance, they might speak up if they see that some children are not getting the same chances as others. They might help organize ways for everyone to have equal access to resources. In this way, Libra's idea of balance goes beyond personal life and extends to the wider world.

Balance does not mean ignoring differences. Libras can recognize that people have unique opinions, skills, and experiences. Instead, balance can mean giving each person space to share those differences. When conflicts happen, a Libra might say, "Let's find a way to work together that includes both sides." This does not guarantee a perfect outcome, but it can open the door to cooperation. The sign's focus on harmony can motivate people to search for solutions that do not leave anyone out.

Some people link balance to mental calm. If your mind is always racing or you worry about many things, you might feel out of balance. Libras might suggest finding a steady approach to thinking. That can include slowing down, writing out pros and cons, or talking it out with a friend. By weighing each concern carefully, you can figure out what is important and what is not. This helps bring mental calm, even if you still have decisions to make.

In daily life, you might see how balance works when you plan your day. You set aside time for homework, time for chores, and time to play or talk with loved ones. You might also keep an eye on healthy eating, making sure you have a mix of foods instead of just one kind. This approach can help keep your body and mind in good shape. For someone with strong Libra traits, it might be second nature to think, "Let's not do too much of just one activity."

Of course, many people, not only Libras, care about balance. Still, Libra stands out in astrology for placing a big spotlight on it. The sign suggests that life is better when things are not extreme. Libras often prefer peaceful methods of resolving conflicts and may work hard to stay calm when faced with tension. They might also encourage others to do the same. This is why Libras can sometimes be known as peacemakers or mediators, although this can be draining if they have to do it too often.

A main idea is that balance is not a one-time event. It is something we try to keep every day. You might wake up and feel balanced, but by the end of the day, tasks have piled up, or you had an argument with a friend. Then you have to find a way to restore that sense of evenness. Libras might remind themselves that it is okay to change plans if it helps things stay fair. They might say, "I wanted to do this project alone, but I see you need help. Let's figure out a fair way to work together."

Sometimes, people think that "balanced" means being bland. But that is not really what Libra energy is about. Instead, it means not going too far in one direction without reason. A Libra might still have strong likes and dislikes, but they try to make sure those likes and dislikes do not harm others or create an unfair situation. They might be open to hearing new ideas, even if they have a preference. That openness is another side of balance: allowing space for different thoughts.

In friendships, balance can show up as giving and receiving support. If one person is always helping and never gets help in return, that friendship can become imbalanced. A Libra might notice that and encourage the group to pitch in. This can help everyone feel included. The same goes for emotional support. Libras might check that their friend's needs are addressed and also remember to share their own feelings. They know that it is not fair if one person always listens while the other never does.

Balance is also important when it comes to taking on new interests. A Libra might say yes to a new club or activity, but then realize they are short on time for other things they enjoy. They might step back and weigh the cost of giving up free time versus the fun of the new activity. This can help them decide whether to continue or drop the activity. Sometimes, Libras can be so eager to keep things fun for everyone that they overschedule themselves, which is another problem. Finding balance can also mean learning to say no sometimes.

Another piece of balance is self-awareness. Libras can look at their own mood and ask if they are feeling calm or if they are too stressed. If they are too stressed, they might set aside time to rest, see friends, or enjoy a quiet hobby. This can help them return to a more balanced state. They might also notice if they are too relaxed and not doing their duties. In that case, they could decide to become more active. Either way, they try to keep an even approach.

All in all, the idea of balance for Libra covers a lot of ground. It touches on how they handle emotions, friendships, work, and leisure time. It also affects how they view disagreements and new ideas. Balancing does not mean everything is always perfect. Rather, it is a steady effort to avoid extremes and find a fair middle. If life is like a scale, Libras aim to keep it from tipping too far. Their symbol of scales and their tie to fairness help them remember that evenness can create a more peaceful atmosphere, both for themselves and for the people around them.

CHAPTER 5: NOTABLE PERSONALITY TRAITS

Many people hear that Libra is about fairness and balance, but there are other qualities linked to this zodiac sign. While not everyone born under Libra will show every trait, there are a few that are often mentioned by those who read about astrology. We can look at these traits in a bit more detail to see how they might shape a Libra's outlook.

One trait that stands out is sociability. Some say Libras often enjoy being around people, whether it is in big groups or small gatherings. They might feel energized when they can chat and share ideas. This does not always mean they are loud. Some Libras can be quiet, but they still appreciate friendly company. They might smile at others and listen to what they have to say, creating a pleasant environment.

Another quality people talk about is the Libra's desire for harmony. This goes beyond just wanting fairness. Libras might prefer to avoid loud arguments, so they try to prevent them from happening. If they sense someone is upset, they may step in to find a peaceful solution. They might gently guide the conversation in a calm direction or suggest taking a break before emotions run too high. This gentle approach can calm tensions before they get worse.

Libras are also often described as polite or courteous. Because they want to keep things peaceful, they might use kind words and show good manners. They may say "please" and "thank you" regularly, opening doors for others or giving compliments. These gestures can help people feel at ease. In some cases, a Libra might go out of their way to ensure everyone is comfortable in a social setting.

Decision-making is another trait that often comes up. Libras can see multiple sides of an issue, which can be good for understanding different perspectives. At the same time, they might take longer to come to a final choice because they do not want to act unfairly. This can lead some Libras to go back and forth, trying to find a perfect solution when one might not exist. Over time, some Libras learn to trust their instincts more, but it can be a challenge.

Patience can be part of a Libra's personality. They might wait before speaking, giving others a chance to share. They could also show patience in situations where someone else might be quick to judge. A Libra might think, "Let's gather more information and learn what everyone needs." This can be helpful in group projects, family talks, or any decision where different people must be heard. However, it can also lead them to delay taking action if they feel they still lack full information.

Many say Libras have an eye for beauty. This does not always mean they must be artists, but they might notice details in their surroundings. A Libra might appreciate a painting, a piece of music, or a tidy arrangement of furniture. They could take pleasure in picking clothing that fits well and looks pleasing. This trait is often connected to their ruling planet, Venus. While not all Libras focus on art, the sense of noticing what is pleasant is often mentioned as a core part of their style.

Another trait is thoughtfulness. Libras might remember small details about friends, like their favorite foods or games. They could use that information to show kindness later, perhaps by bringing a friend's favorite snack or suggesting an activity they know their friend loves. This thoughtfulness can make Libras appear caring. It ties back to their wish to make people feel acknowledged.

Libras can also be quite diplomatic. This means they may handle disagreements in a way that respects each side. They might avoid strong language that could offend someone. Instead, they try to phrase things gently. If two people are arguing, a Libra might say, "I hear your point, and I also understand the other side. Is there a way we can meet in the middle?" This does not mean Libras never get angry, but they might calm themselves before speaking, hoping to avoid escalating tension.

Another personality trait we can consider is adaptability. Libras might be flexible when plans change, especially if they believe a new plan could suit everyone better. They may be open to suggestions and might not insist on doing things only their way. In some cases, this can be a strength, as it allows them to cooperate smoothly with others. However, if they adapt too much, they might lose track of their own preferences. Finding a balance between being flexible and standing firm is an ongoing task for many Libras.

A potential challenge for Libras is overthinking. Because they can see many sides to a problem, they might get stuck in their thoughts, examining every possibility. This can slow down their actions or lead them to seek too many opinions. Friends might say, "Just pick something!" if a Libra takes too long to make a choice. Overthinking can also bring anxiety if they worry about letting people down.

Libras may display optimism. They might look for the bright side of a situation and hope for the best. This positive outlook can help them bring confidence into group settings. If a problem arises, they might believe that by talking it out and being fair, a solution can be found. Not every Libra will have a strong sense of optimism, but many are known to try to keep spirits up with pleasant conversation or small acts of kindness.

Empathy is another trait people connect with Libra. Because Libras pay attention to fairness, they often think about how others feel.

They might pick up on subtle cues that someone is unhappy or worried. A Libra might approach that person quietly and ask if they want to talk. They could offer a supportive word or a gentle suggestion. This empathy can help them form deep friendships because people appreciate the understanding they show.

Some Libras might have a playful side. They enjoy laughter and lighthearted jokes, especially when the environment is positive. They might crack a friendly joke to ease tension if they sense conflict. Their desire for harmony could lead them to use humor as a way to bring people together. If done well, this can brighten the mood; if done at the wrong time, it might not always help. Still, many Libras seem to have a knack for knowing when to slip in a playful remark.

Another interesting quality is a love of conversation. Libras might like to talk about many topics, from the latest events to personal interests. They enjoy hearing different points of view. This social side can make them good company in discussions. However, they typically prefer calm talks rather than heated debates. They may try to keep the tone friendly and avoid letting the discussion turn into a shouting match.

Some also speak of Libras having a balanced sense of self. They might not want to brag too much, nor do they want to fade into the background. Finding that middle ground can help them appear poised and self-assured without seeming proud. This trait might show in how they stand, speak, or carry themselves. It could also show in how they encourage others to share the spotlight.

Creativity can appear in Libras who have an artistic streak. This might not be universal, but many feel drawn to creative hobbies like drawing, music, or writing. They might enjoy these activities as a way to add beauty to the world or to channel their ideas. Even if a Libra is not an artist, they might still have creative solutions to problems. Their ability to see multiple angles can help them come up with new approaches that others miss.

Another trait often linked to Libras is a sense of fairness toward themselves. They might realize if they are overworking or being too hard on themselves. Then, they try to step back and allow some rest or self-care. On the other hand, if they realize they have been ignoring a task, they might gently push themselves to catch up. This self-check can be useful, but it depends on how practiced they are at noticing their own patterns.

Libras might also enjoy activities that involve teamwork. They might feel it is more fun to do things as a group, whether it is playing a sport, creating a group presentation, or putting on a small show at school. They might assume the role of organizer who checks that everyone is getting along. This can make them natural team players or group leaders, but they must watch out for the stress that can come from always trying to keep the peace.

A drawback that sometimes goes along with wanting harmony is avoidance. A Libra might avoid issues that need addressing because they do not like conflict. Instead of speaking up early, they could wait until the matter grows bigger. Over time, they might learn that being direct can prevent bigger troubles later. But in early experiences, Libras might hold back to keep things calm on the surface, even if it means ignoring a real concern.

Honesty is another area that can be interesting for Libras. Because they want to be polite and kind, they might soften their words. This does not necessarily mean they are dishonest; rather, they may phrase the truth in a gentle way. For instance, if a friend wants feedback on a project, a Libra might find positive things to say before pointing out any problems. This soft honesty can keep friends from feeling hurt, but sometimes the friend might need more direct critique. Striking the right balance between kindness and honesty can be a Libra lesson.

Libras can also carry a desire to learn about others. They might ask many questions to understand someone's background or interests. This curiosity can foster good relationships. They might be open to hearing about different cultures, viewpoints, or hobbies. However, if they encounter someone who is closed off or who becomes aggressive, a Libra might step away rather than fight. They often prefer understanding and respect over confrontation.

Forward planning can also be a Libra characteristic. Some Libras like to list out all the tasks they need to do, scheduling them so they do not feel rushed later. They might do this to keep their life calm and under control. However, if something unexpected comes up, they can adapt—provided they remember to stay flexible. Their fondness for planning is often linked to their wish to avoid sudden chaos or stress.

When we look at these personality traits as a whole, we see that Libras are generally seen as calm, fair-minded, empathetic, and social individuals who try hard to keep things pleasant. They can be quite sweet in how they approach people, but they might struggle with decisions and sometimes avoid conflict. They appreciate charm and kindness, and they may show a natural concern for others' feelings.

Of course, not every Libra will display all these traits in the same way. People can be shaped by family life, personal experiences, and many other factors. Still, these common themes give an overall picture of what people usually think when they describe Libra personalities. It might be summarized as "friendly, polite, and balanced," with a gentle approach to life's ups and downs.

CHAPTER 6: LIBRA AND FRIENDSHIPS

Friendships are an important part of life for many Libras. They tend to enjoy spending time with people, sharing thoughts, and working together on projects. In this chapter, we will look more deeply at how a Libra might act in friendships and group settings, and why fairness plays a big role.

First, Libras often look for harmony in their social circles. They might want everyone to get along and have a good time. When friends are talking, a Libra may step in if they notice someone getting cut off or ignored. The Libra might say, "Wait, let's hear what you have to say," giving the quieter friend a chance to speak. This helps keep the conversation balanced.

Many Libras place a strong value on kindness. They may make an effort to remember birthdays or ask how a friend is doing when they seem sad. If a friend is worried about a test at school, the Libra might offer to help study or just provide a listening ear. In this way, Libras can be seen as caring friends who make others feel important.

Because Libras prefer peaceful chats, they might steer the group away from arguments. If two friends have a disagreement, the Libra might sit down with each person separately, trying to see how they feel. Then, they might bring them together and say, "It sounds like you both want a fair solution. Can we find one that works for everyone?" This kind of mediation can keep friendship groups running smoothly. However, it does mean Libras may sometimes feel pressure to fix problems, which can be tiring.

In group activities, Libras are known for being team players. They often check if everyone is comfortable with the plan. They might say, "Are we sure everyone is okay with meeting on Saturday?" or "Does anyone else have a better idea?" By doing this, they help the group feel heard. It can also make the group's final choice more balanced, which is a big deal for Libras.

Another aspect of Libra friendships is the importance of shared respect. A Libra generally does not like it if a friend speaks rudely or treats someone unfairly. They might feel uneasy if they see bullying or harsh teasing. In that case, they could step in quietly or talk to the friend in private, explaining why the behavior is hurtful. Libras might not like direct confrontation, but they also dislike injustice, so they might find a calm way to address it.

Libras tend to be good listeners. They might look a friend in the eye, nod, and ask questions. This makes the friend feel heard. In many friendships, people appreciate having someone who will truly listen. Libras often do well at this because they enjoy learning different perspectives. They also want to make sure the friend feels understood before they offer any advice or feedback.

A common challenge is that Libras sometimes avoid telling friends when they are upset, in order to keep the peace. If a friend does something that hurts them, a Libra might stay quiet to prevent conflict. Over time, this can cause hidden tension. It might be healthier for the Libra to speak up early in a polite way, saying, "It bothered me when you did that. Can we talk about it?" That way, they can resolve issues before they grow bigger.

Another point is how Libras handle group outings. They might spend time asking everyone where they want to go or what they want to eat, trying to include all opinions. This can be helpful, but if the group is large, it can become tricky. Some friends might say, "Just pick something!" A Libra can struggle with that if they worry about choosing a plan that not everyone likes. Over time, a Libra may learn to offer a few fair options instead of trying to please everyone all at once.

Libras may also bring a sense of fun to friendships, especially in relaxed settings. They might suggest playing games that require teamwork or sharing funny stories. Because they like a pleasant atmosphere, they might avoid games that are too competitive or that can lead to arguing. They usually enjoy activities that leave most people smiling at the end.

Trust can be a key element of Libra's friendships. Since Libras often show care and concern for fairness, they might expect their friends to do the same. If a friend breaks trust, the Libra could feel more hurt than others might. They might feel as though the person did not respect the basic idea of treating each other fairly. If that happens, Libras might find it hard to move on unless they have a real talk about what went wrong.

Libras often enjoy sharing. If they have a snack or an interesting book, they might offer it to a friend. They do not like seeing a friend left out. This trait of sharing can make them popular in friend groups, as others know that a Libra is likely to be generous with both items and time. Sometimes, though, Libras should remember not to overextend themselves. They must keep a balance between giving to friends and saving enough energy and resources for themselves.

Another tendency is that Libras might want everything to be nice in the group, so if there is a serious issue, they may try to lighten it too quickly. For example, if a friend is deeply sad, a Libra may try to joke around to help them feel better. While kind, this approach might skip over the friend's real need to express serious emotions. So, Libras may need to practice understanding when it is time to just listen and not rush to make things "all good" right away.

In some cases, Libras enjoy matching friends who might get along. For instance, if a Libra knows two people who share similar interests, they might introduce them. The Libra might say, "You both love drawing, so maybe you can draw together sometime." This can help the Libra's social circle grow and stay connected. They might be like a friendly link between different groups.

Libras can also bring fairness to group tasks. If a group assignment is divided among team members, a Libra may try to ensure each person has a role that they can handle without feeling overwhelmed. They might ask, "Does everyone have a task they are okay with?" or "Are we sharing the work evenly?" This can improve teamwork and lower the chance of someone feeling resentful. The Libra's focus on fairness helps keep the effort balanced.

Because Libras can be diplomatic, they might occasionally act as a go-between for two friends who are not speaking to each other. This can be helpful, but it can also be a lot of stress. The Libra might feel they are stuck in the middle, trying to keep both sides happy. If the conflict is big, a Libra might need to set limits, saying they cannot solve the whole problem themselves. Otherwise, they risk burning out from trying to fix something that only the two friends can truly resolve.

Libras tend to be open-minded about new people joining the group. They might not want a friend circle to become closed off. They could say, "Sure, bring your friend along. More people can mean more fun!" Because Libras like peace, they might want to welcome newcomers in a polite way, hoping to keep the social vibe positive.

When new people arrive, the Libra might introduce them properly so they do not feel alone.

Another interesting aspect is that Libras might sometimes try to avoid negative feedback. If a friend has done something wrong, a Libra might wait for someone else to point it out. They do not want to be the one to create tension. But this can be a problem if no one else speaks up. Then, the friend might never learn how their actions hurt others. In time, Libras can see that direct but gentle honesty can be more helpful than silent acceptance.

Libras in friendships often value shared experiences. They might enjoy small traditions, like meeting regularly for a meal or a game. They like the stability such activities can bring, as it strengthens the bond. They might plan events where everyone can do something they like. This could be a simple backyard hangout or a walk in the park. The key for the Libra is that no one is left feeling bored or overlooked.

Many Libras believe that even if two friends have different opinions, there is usually a way to find common ground. For example, if one friend loves sports while another loves reading, a Libra might suggest an activity that has a bit of both, or at least make sure each interest is respected by the group. This openness can help a Libra group of friends be diverse and still stay connected.

A possible pitfall is that Libras might get worn out if they have too many friendships to maintain. Because they do not want to let anyone down, they might keep saying yes to gatherings or tasks, leaving no free time for themselves. Over time, they might feel overstretched. This can lead to stress or resentment. A healthy Libra will learn to set boundaries, politely telling friends they need a quiet day or that they cannot join every event.

In one-on-one friendships, a Libra might be supportive and encouraging, asking the friend about their goals and offering help. They might check in with text messages or small notes, wanting to keep the connection strong. Their polite and gentle nature can make them a comfort to friends. However, if the friend is very forceful or demanding, the Libra may need to speak up to avoid being pushed around.

Libras might also be drawn to friends who share similar values of fairness. If a friend constantly makes rude comments about others or acts selfishly, that might clash with a Libra's principles. The Libra could try to stay polite, but deep down, they might sense the friendship is not good for them. Since Libras often avoid conflict, it can take a while for them to step back. When they do, they may do so quietly, without a big confrontation.

In summary, friendships for Libras tend to revolve around kindness, politeness, and equality. Libras try to ensure that everyone's voice is heard and that no one is left feeling unimportant. They bring a gentle approach to social situations, looking for ways to keep the group happy. This can make them valuable friends who can smooth out small problems before they escalate. But it can also place stress on the Libra if they feel responsible for everyone's comfort.

Overall, a Libra's friendships reflect their core traits. They often show warmth, understanding, and a readiness to share. They might work behind the scenes to maintain peace among friends. As long as they remember to speak up for themselves and not shoulder every conflict alone, Libras can form strong, lasting bonds that benefit both them and the people they care about.

CHAPTER 7: LIBRA AND ROMANCE

Romance is a topic many people think about when reading about astrology. Every sign is said to have a certain way of expressing affection, handling relationship challenges, and bonding with a partner. Libra is often linked to qualities like harmony, fairness, and care for others. Because of this, many believe Libras are well suited for warm, respectful relationships. This chapter will look at how Libras might approach romantic connections, including how they express affection, how they prefer to handle disagreements, and why fairness is so important to them in matters of the heart.

A Friendly Start

Many Libras begin their romantic relationships by forming a bond that feels friendly and balanced. They may not rush into deep feelings right away. Instead, they might want to learn about a person's hobbies, experiences, and character. Because Libra is an air sign, talking and sharing ideas can be the doorway to closer feelings. A Libra might meet someone and think, "This person seems interesting. Let me find out more," before deciding whether they feel a stronger spark.

This friendly start can give a Libra time to see if the person's values match their own. Does this new individual treat others with respect? Do they show kindness to friends or strangers? Since Libras value fairness and politeness, they will notice behavior that seems rude or hurtful. If they see signs that the person is too harsh, they might step back. But if the person displays warmth and courtesy, the Libra is more likely to move forward.

Charm and Attraction

In astrology, Libra is linked to Venus, which is often seen as the planet of beauty, affection, and comfort. Because of this connection, Libras might show a certain charm in how they talk or act. They can be gentle in their words, often using polite phrases or compliments. When they are interested in someone, they tend to show it by being supportive and listening carefully to that person's thoughts.

If a Libra likes someone's sense of humor, they may smile or laugh easily during a conversation. They might remember small details the person shares and bring those details up later. For example, if the person mentions they love a certain type of cookie, the Libra might surprise them with that treat next time they meet. These thoughtful acts can be a sign of the Libra's growing affection.

At the same time, Libras enjoy feeling that they are in a pleasant, comfortable space when romance is budding. They might pick a calm coffee shop or a quiet park for their first outings. The atmosphere matters because Libras want to avoid loud conflicts or tense vibes. A soft, relaxed environment helps them and their partner feel at ease.

Focus on Harmony

One of the biggest themes for Libra in romance is harmony. Libras often want to get along with their partner without constant disagreements. That does not mean they expect zero conflict; no relationship is perfect. But they do try to prevent tiny issues from growing bigger. If a small misunderstanding arises, a Libra may say, "Let's talk about it now rather than later," hoping to fix it gently.

This focus on harmony also shows in how Libras might handle routine tasks with a partner. They might prefer splitting chores so that each person feels the division is fair. For instance, a Libra might say, "I will cook dinner if you can help wash the dishes afterward," or "We can both clean the living room so it does not feel like one person is doing more." They believe sharing tasks is a key way to keep the relationship balanced. If one side feels taken for granted, it can lead to resentment, which Libras aim to avoid.

Decision-Making Together

In romance, one challenge Libras often face is making decisions. Libras like to weigh all sides of a choice, which can be helpful, but it can also slow things down. In a relationship, decisions come up all the time: where to go on a weekend, what furniture to buy, how to handle a shared budget, and so on. A Libra might ask their partner many questions to make sure the choice is fair and that both people's preferences are considered.

Sometimes, a partner may say, "It's okay, you pick this time." If the Libra still struggles to pick, it can be because they do not want to make a decision that leaves the partner unhappy later. They might say, "I want to be sure you will like this place for dinner," or "Are you truly fine with me choosing the movie?" This can come across as indecision, but it is often a way of being thoughtful. Over time, Libras might become more comfortable making choices if they sense their partner genuinely trusts them to decide.

Expressing Feelings

Libras can be gentle in sharing their feelings. They might not shout their love from the rooftops on day one, but they show affection in smaller, caring ways. For example, they may write a nice note, remember an important date, or give heartfelt compliments. They might also express affection by creating a pleasing setting for time together, such as setting up a cozy dinner at home with soft music.

However, Libras can sometimes hold back their deeper worries or annoyances to keep things calm. This means if they feel hurt, they might delay telling their partner. They do this to avoid arguments, but this can lead to misunderstandings. If the partner never hears the Libra's concerns, they might repeat a behavior that bothers the Libra. Over time, Libras can learn that polite honesty is better than allowing issues to build up.

Romance as a Team Effort

For Libras, a romantic relationship is often seen as a team effort rather than a clash of wills. They like the idea that both partners support each other equally. A Libra might say, "We succeed together, and we face challenges together," rather than "I'm on my own, and you're on your own." They want to share life's ups and downs in a balanced way.

When problems arise, Libras tend to look for solutions that do not overlook either person's needs. They might ask, "What do you need right now, and what do I need? How can we meet in the middle?" Because of this, they might be good at working through small quarrels calmly, as they try not to dismiss the partner's viewpoint. Still, they can get stuck if they see too many possible compromises. They might say, "We could do it this way, or that way, or maybe another way," struggling to finalize a path forward.

Thoughtfulness and Small Gestures

Many Libras show their love by paying attention to small details. They might recall which flowers their partner likes or plan a surprise that reflects the partner's interests. They may take note of the partner's favorite songs, foods, or movies, then bring those into shared activities. This care for detail can make the partner feel valued. It also aligns with Libra's sense of fairness: "If you share parts of yourself with me, I will remember and honor them."

These little gestures can be a big part of Libra romance. A Libra might send a kind text during the day to check in, pick up a snack the partner enjoys, or plan a pleasant walk at a spot they know the partner loves. These actions can seem simple, but they reflect the Libra's desire to keep the relationship warm and balanced.

Handling Conflict with Poise

No matter how peaceful Libras want things, disagreements and arguments will happen in most relationships. A Libra might try to prevent the situation from becoming loud. For instance, if voices start rising, they could say, "Let's take a moment to breathe and talk calmly." They believe that once anger is too high, it can be hard to have a productive conversation.

Sometimes Libras can overdo this, brushing aside real concerns to keep the peace. If the other person is upset, ignoring that upset feeling just to avoid conflict might make things worse over time. A balanced approach for Libra is to listen closely to the partner's complaints, acknowledge them, and then talk about solutions in a respectful tone. If both people feel heard, the Libra's desire for harmony can be met without shutting down important discussions.

Fairness and Give-and-Take

In romantic connections, Libras often want a sense of give-and-take. This means they do not like relationships where one side takes charge all the time or always makes all the decisions. They also do not enjoy a setup where one person does all the emotional labor—listening, comforting, planning—while the other person does little. Fairness is so vital to Libras that if they notice an ongoing imbalance, they can become unhappy.

When a Libra sees that they are giving more than they are receiving, they might start to feel disrespected. Yet, they might hesitate to speak up immediately to avoid sounding selfish. Over time, however, their hurt can grow, and they may finally express it. A more balanced path is for the Libra to communicate sooner, saying, "I feel like I'm doing a lot of the emotional work. Can we find a better way to share it?" This direct conversation can protect the relationship from building hidden resentments.

Romantic Surprises and Beauty

Because Libra is guided by Venus, many believe Libras appreciate beauty and may enjoy creating a pleasing mood. This can show up in romance through thoughtful surprises. A Libra might plan a special date with soft lighting, gentle music, and a nice meal. They may choose a park with pretty views or decorate a room with items that reflect their partner's taste.

These efforts are not always extravagant. Even small touches—like placing a fresh flower on the table—can matter to a Libra. They want the moment to feel calm, warm, and inviting. This sense of atmosphere often helps the Libra feel more comfortable expressing affection, which in turn can help their partner feel cherished.

Slow to Show Anger

When it comes to strong negative emotions, Libras might keep things in for a while because they dislike arguments. If something is truly bothering them, they might try hinting at it gently. If the partner does not pick up on the hint, the Libra might become increasingly frustrated. Finally, they could burst out with anger they have held back. This can surprise the partner, who might have thought everything was fine.

Learning healthy ways to express anger or frustration is important for Libras. They do not have to be rude or loud, but direct communication helps. Saying, "I feel hurt when this happens," is more effective than hoping the partner will guess. This is an ongoing lesson for Libras: balancing politeness with honest expression of negative emotions.

Long-Term Commitment

If a Libra decides they want a long-term relationship or marriage, they often approach it with serious thought. They consider whether their partner's values match theirs, whether the daily routines will remain fair, and whether both can work together as a team. Because they want stability and equality, they might talk with their partner about finances, chores, and family expectations before taking a big step. This can be a good thing, because open discussion can prevent future misunderstandings.

Some Libras might wait a while before fully committing, not because they are fearful of love, but because they want to make sure they are making a fair and balanced choice. They may also want to be confident that their partner is equally invested. Once they do commit, Libras often try hard to keep the partnership healthy, using their skills at compromise to navigate any rough patches.

Romance and Social Circles

Because Libras are often sociable, they enjoy introducing their partner to friends and attending gatherings as a couple. They might feel proud to show off the person they care about. They also want to see how their partner interacts with the important people in their life. If their friends like the partner, that can feel very reassuring to a Libra. Likewise, if the partner shows warmth and respect to the friend group, the Libra might feel more confident in the bond.

However, Libras may worry if the partner seems unfriendly or dismissive to their friends. Since Libras see friends as a big part of their life, they want harmony between their partner and their social group. A Libra might try to mediate if tension arises, looking for a fair explanation. They could say, "I know you did not mean to offend my friend, but maybe you can talk it out so everyone feels better."

Sticking Up for Their Partner

In many cases, Libras who value fairness will defend their loved ones if they see them being mistreated. Even though Libras do not love conflict, they can become quite firm if a friend or relative is unkind to their partner. They might say calmly but clearly, "That is not acceptable. Let's talk about this with respect." Libras do not want to see their partner hurt, especially in a setting where no one else is speaking up. This protective side can show that Libras do have limits; they will take a stand if they feel a situation is unjust.

Potential Struggles in Libra Romance

While there are many positive traits Libras bring to romance, there can be struggles:

- **Over-reliance on harmony:** A Libra might skip talking about problems because they want the relationship to feel peaceful. This can backfire when hidden issues burst out later.
- **Indecision:** Libras can have a hard time with major choices, from what home to rent or buy, to whether to move in together. This can be frustrating for a partner who likes quick decisions.
- **Pleasing everyone:** If the Libra tries to please not just their partner but also a wide circle of friends and family, they might spread themselves too thin. This can cause stress, leaving the partner feeling neglected.
- **Fear of conflict:** Though many people dislike conflict, Libras might let issues slide longer than they should. A more balanced approach is to address disagreements gently but promptly.

Being aware of these struggles can help a Libra and their partner avoid bigger challenges. Good communication and understanding can address most of these points over time.

Encouraging a Libra in Love

If you are in a relationship with a Libra or if you are a friend to a Libra who is exploring a new romance, you can help them by encouraging open dialogue. You might say, "It is okay to voice your dislikes or opinions. You will not cause a huge argument by being honest." This reassurance can help a Libra feel safe expressing themselves. It also helps them learn that disagreements do not always ruin relationships; they can actually make the connection stronger if handled in a caring way.

Showing gratitude for their gestures also goes a long way. Libras like to know that their efforts at fairness and kindness are noticed. A simple "Thank you for thinking of me" or "I appreciate how you always consider my feelings" can make them feel valued, encouraging them to keep the balance they treasure.

Navigating Modern Romance

In today's world, romantic relationships can take many forms, from in-person dating to online connections. Libras tend to adapt well to various styles as long as mutual respect is present. They might enjoy online chats that allow them to exchange thoughtful messages, exploring each other's ideas. However, they might also want face-to-face time eventually, because reading a person's tone and body language can be important for them. They want to sense the "vibe" and ensure it feels polite and genuine.

On social media, Libras might share posts or pictures that look balanced and visually appealing, reflecting their love of harmony. They might also be careful about how they comment or respond to their partner's posts, aiming to remain supportive and kind. If they see drama unfolding online, they may try to stay out of it or resolve it quietly rather than jump into a loud fight.

Dealing with Breakups

Breakups are painful for anyone, and Libras are no exception. Because they invest so much in maintaining a sense of peace, a breakup can feel like the collapse of something they worked hard to keep balanced. They might go through phases of self-blame, wondering if they should have compromised more or shared their true feelings sooner. They may also look back at the relationship and see all the small steps they took to keep things fair, which can deepen their sadness.

However, once a Libra realizes the relationship ended for reasons that could not be fixed, they might find calm in focusing on self-care and reflection. They could decide to spend time with supportive friends or family. Over time, they might look back and identify areas where they can grow, such as speaking up sooner or asking for their needs to be met. The Libra's ability to see multiple sides of a situation can help them learn from the experience, though it can also cause them to linger on the "what ifs."

Rebounding and Finding New Love

After a breakup, some Libras might quickly seek a new connection. This is not always due to being shallow; rather, Libras often feel best when they can share experiences with someone else. They might miss the sense of balance that partnership gives them. However, if they jump in too fast, they risk not taking enough time to heal and figure out what went wrong in the old relationship. So, a Libra who wants a healthy new start should take a bit of time to reflect. They can ask themselves, "What would I like to do differently next time?" or "How can I share my thoughts more openly?"

When they are ready, Libras tend to bring their gentle approach to new potential partners. They might be open to meeting through friends or going on group outings first, especially if they are shy about diving into a one-on-one setting right away. They also might compare new people's traits to what they have learned is important to them: kindness, fairness, and a friendly spirit.

Libra's Romantic Compatibility

Some people are curious about which signs Libra might get along with romantically. While astrology can offer suggestions, real relationships depend on the personalities of both individuals. Traditionally, Libras are said to get along well with other air signs (Gemini and Aquarius) because of shared interests in talking and thinking. Libra might also do well with fire signs (Aries, Leo, Sagittarius), who can bring excitement and warmth, though this can sometimes lead to conflicts if the fire sign is too direct and the Libra is too conflict-avoidant. Earth signs (Taurus, Virgo, Capricorn) might give Libras stability, but the Libra might need to practice open communication to bridge differences in approach. Water signs (Cancer, Scorpio, Pisces) can offer emotional depth, though the Libra might need to ensure that negative feelings do not go unspoken on either side.

Of course, these are just broad ideas. Many Libras can find loving partnerships with signs that do not fit the usual "best match." True compatibility depends on a variety of factors, including life experiences, personal values, and the willingness of both people to grow together.

Romance as an Ongoing Process

For Libras, romance is not a simple once-and-done event. It is more of an ongoing act of balancing two people's needs, dreams, and quirks. Each day, the couple might face new questions: "Who will do the grocery shopping?" "How do we handle stress from work or school?" "What do we want for our future?" A Libra typically tries to address these questions with fairness in mind, aiming to include the partner's voice at every step.

Over time, Libras may refine their approach to romance. In youth, they might rely heavily on politeness and harmony, sometimes neglecting their own needs. As they grow, they learn that healthy relationships include open communication of each person's wants and boundaries. The more they practice speaking honestly, the better their chances of forming a well-balanced relationship that benefits both partners.

Sharing Hobbies and Interests

One aspect of Libra romance is the desire to share fun activities. Libras often enjoy doing things that let them connect with their partner in a friendly, relaxed way. This could be visiting art museums, attending small concerts, going for nature walks, or even taking a simple cooking class together. The key is that both people can chat, collaborate, or appreciate something together. Libras like to keep experiences inclusive, so if the partner has a particular hobby, they might try it out to show support.

Equally, Libras might introduce their own interests gently, checking if the partner is open to them. For instance, if a Libra likes reading about different cultures, they might ask if the partner wants to explore a local cultural festival. It is all about combining tastes so both sides feel involved. This sense of shared enjoyment can strengthen the bond.

Balancing Romance and Independence

Even though Libras love togetherness, they also understand that people need personal time. They might encourage their partner to keep hobbies or friendships outside the relationship, as long as it is done with respect and communication. Libras can feel uneasy if they see their partner drifting too far into separate pursuits, but they also do not want to smother them. It is a balancing act: giving each other enough space to be individuals while still coming together for shared moments.

A Libra might say, "I love doing things with you, but I also think it's good if we each have our own outlets." That way, they avoid codependence, where both partners rely only on each other for all needs. At the same time, Libra might like a routine check-in: "How was your day? Did you have fun at your hobby group?" This keeps the lines of communication open so both people feel connected.

Growth Over Time

As a Libra's romantic life progresses, growth happens through shared experiences, conflicts resolved, and joys celebrated. Each milestone—like deciding to move in together, meeting each other's families, or taking a trip—can add layers of understanding. Libras might keep seeking new ways to maintain fairness, such as rotating who plans dates or splitting financial responsibilities in a way that feels good to both.

If the relationship faces a serious test—like a long-distance situation, health issues, or family stress—Libras will try to solve it through honest talks and a spirit of cooperation. They might say, "Let's figure out how we can both feel heard and supported during this tough time," rather than letting one person shoulder the entire burden. This is where the Libra's diplomatic skill can shine, assuming the partner also values working together.

CHAPTER 8: LIBRA AND FAMILY TIES

Family relationships can have a big impact on how Libras learn about fairness, communication, and handling conflicts. From parents and siblings to extended relatives, the family circle provides a space where a Libra's balance-seeking nature can shine—or be tested. In this chapter, we will explore how Libras tend to interact within their families, how they might handle disagreements at home, and what strategies they use to maintain harmony. We will also discuss the challenges Libras can face when family members have clashing opinions or when expectations are high.

Early Lessons on Fairness

Many Libras say their sense of fairness shows up early in life. If they have siblings, they might notice how chores, treats, or privileges are shared. A Libra child might ask, "Why does my brother get to stay up later than I do?" or "Why am I always the one washing dishes?" They want to understand the reasoning behind rules and see if they are applied evenly.

If parents explain things clearly—like saying the older sibling has extra school responsibilities, so they get different bedtimes—then the Libra might accept it more easily. But if rules seem random or favor one child unfairly, a young Libra can feel upset. This can be a first step in shaping the Libra's belief that things should be balanced at home.

Polite Peacemaker

In many families, there can be small arguments, such as disagreements about what to eat for dinner, where to go on vacation, or who does which chores. A Libra might become the peacemaker who tries to calm everyone down. Even as a child or teen, they may say, "Let's listen to each other's ideas," hoping to find a solution that everyone can accept.

This peacemaking role can be helpful for keeping family bonds strong, but it can also put pressure on the Libra. They might feel responsible for solving conflicts that are not really theirs to fix. For example, if two siblings are always fighting, the Libra might jump in to mediate. Over time, they could grow stressed from dealing with constant bickering. Learning boundaries becomes important, so the Libra does not feel like they must fix every issue.

Bonding with Parents

Libras typically want a friendly bond with their parents or guardians. They appreciate gentle conversations rather than harsh lectures. If a parent is strict but fair, the Libra might respect them. However, if a parent seems to play favorites or scolds without listening, the Libra might withdraw. They might not lash out openly, but they could feel less inclined to share their thoughts.

Because Libras often communicate politely, a Libra child might be the one who tries to speak calmly even when the parent is upset. They may say, "I understand you are angry, but can we talk this through?" This approach can sometimes ease tension. On the other hand, if a parent dismisses the child's attempt at respectful discussion, the Libra might become quiet and hide their feelings in order to avoid further conflict.

Cooperation and Chores

At home, chores and tasks can become a test of fairness. Libras will notice if one family member seems to do more than the others. They might say, "It does not feel right that I do all the laundry while someone else never helps." If the family sets up a schedule or a clear method of splitting tasks, it can satisfy the Libra's wish for balance. They will likely do their share willingly, as long as they see that everyone else is also contributing.

If chores are not distributed fairly, a Libra might try to bring it up in a calm way. "I have been doing the dishes all week. Maybe we can rotate so that each person does it on different days?" This is a typical Libra approach: suggest a system that feels just to everyone. If the family agrees, the Libra feels validated. If the family shrugs them off, the Libra could become quietly frustrated, which might eventually lead to a bigger emotional outburst.

Family Gatherings

Extended family gatherings—such as holiday meals or other get-togethers—can be both fun and stressful for Libras. On one hand, Libras usually like social situations where people can talk and share stories. They enjoy catching up with relatives, hearing about their lives, and sharing updates about their own. On the other hand, large family events can sometimes include strong personalities or old arguments. A Libra might sense tension, like an older relative who disagrees with another relative about politics or lifestyle choices.

A Libra in this setting may try to keep the peace. They might steer the conversation toward neutral topics or try to find common ground: "Yes, we have different opinions, but we all care about each other, right?" If a disagreement becomes heated, the Libra might gently suggest taking a break or shifting focus to something more lighthearted. Sometimes, family members appreciate this calming approach. Other times, they may continue to argue, leaving the Libra feeling upset or drained.

Respect for Traditions, But Not at Any Cost

Some families have traditions that go back generations, like certain ways of celebrating events, certain recipes, or certain roles assigned to different members. Libras can enjoy these traditions, especially if they bring everyone together in a harmonious way. They may like the pleasant atmosphere and the chance to connect with relatives in a structured setting.

However, if a family tradition seems unfair—maybe it favors one branch of the family or excludes certain relatives—a Libra might question it. They could ask, "Do we have to keep doing it this way if it hurts someone's feelings?" Because Libras value respect, they might suggest modifying the tradition to be more welcoming. This can cause friction if older relatives cling to the old ways. But the Libra's intention is usually to make sure no one feels left out or slighted.

Sibling Dynamics

When it comes to siblings, Libras might experience close bonds or frequent disagreements, depending on personalities. If a sibling is also calm and open to sharing, the Libra might have a best-friend-like connection with them, exchanging advice and confiding in each other. The two siblings might back each other up if there is stress in the family, and the Libra's fairness can help them both share chores or plan fun activities together.

If a sibling is more fiery or less interested in balance, the Libra might struggle to keep arguments from flaring. They could try to reason with the sibling and end up feeling that nothing works. Over time, a

Libra might learn to set limits, telling the sibling, "I care about you, but I cannot be your peacekeeper all the time." Though Libra wants harmony, sometimes they have to accept that certain relatives might not change their ways.

Grandparents and Older Relatives

In many families, grandparents or older relatives can hold strong opinions or follow old-fashioned ways of thinking. Libras often approach these elders with politeness, asking questions about their experiences and showing interest in family history. They might appreciate hearing stories of how things used to be. However, if an older relative says something that conflicts with modern values (such as making unfair statements about certain groups of people), the Libra can feel torn. They want to be respectful, yet they also care about fairness and kindness to all.

In such cases, a Libra might respond gently, trying not to cause a big fight but also not wanting to ignore remarks they find hurtful. They could say, "I see you grew up in a different time, but I think we should treat everyone with respect." This balancing act can be hard. If the older relative becomes defensive, the Libra might switch to a polite silence or try to change the subject to avoid a huge conflict. Inside, they could feel uncomfortable. This is where the Libra's nature to keep peace can clash with their desire for fairness to everyone.

Handling Childhood Disagreements

During childhood or the teen years, Libras might see conflicts between adults in the family. This can happen if parents have loud arguments or if extended relatives do not get along. A young Libra might feel anxious watching people they love fight. They could try to step in with words that seem wise beyond their years: "Can we sit down and talk calmly?" They might even offer suggestions for a compromise, surprising adults with their maturity.

While this can be helpful, it also places the child in a tough spot. They might feel a sense of responsibility for the family's peace that is not entirely theirs. If adults rely on the Libra child to "make things better," it can become a heavy emotional load. In the future, that child might become extra sensitive to any sign of conflict at home. Growing up, they could carry the same pattern into other areas of life, always feeling like they have to be the one who fixes everything.

Libra as a Parent

When Libras become parents themselves, they often aim to create a balanced environment for their children. They might set up fair rules, ensuring that each child knows what to expect. They also want to listen to the child's viewpoint, giving them space to explain themselves if they break a rule or if they want to propose something new.

A Libra parent might say, "Let's talk about why you did that. I want to hear your side before I decide on any consequences." This open-minded approach can help build trust. At the same time, Libras must be careful not to waver too much in front of their children. If the child sees that a parent keeps changing rules or cannot make a firm decision, it can cause confusion. So the Libra parent might need to find a way to stay consistent while still hearing the child's voice.

Family Communication Styles

Different families have different ways of communicating. Some families talk loudly and openly about their feelings. Others might keep emotions more private. Libras generally prefer a balanced style, where people can share viewpoints without yelling or name-calling.

If they grow up in a family that does not offer this environment, they might feel stressed.

As adults, Libras might encourage a more relaxed, polite way of talking to each other. They could say, "We can discuss big problems without raising our voices. Let's go step by step." This is part of how they bring fairness into family life: by giving each person a turn to speak and trying to minimize tension. If other relatives continue using harsh language, the Libra might withdraw or attempt to diffuse the situation quietly.

Conflict Over Life Choices

As Libras grow up, they might face family expectations about their choices—such as career path, where to live, or when to start their own family. If the family tries to push them in a direction that does not feel fair or aligned with their wishes, Libras can feel a tug-of-war. They do not want to upset their relatives, but they also want to do what is right for themselves.

They might handle this by attempting to reason with the family. For instance, if the family wants them to stay close by, but the Libra has a job offer far away, the Libra might say, "I understand it's hard for you, but this job might give me a better future. Can we figure out a way to keep in touch and still respect each other's needs?" They hope to find a middle path. If the relatives refuse to compromise, the Libra might quietly follow their own path anyway, feeling sad they could not get full support.

Blended Families and Step-Relatives

In modern life, many families are blended, meaning step-parents, step-siblings, or half-siblings might come into the picture. A Libra in such a setup often tries to smooth the transition. They might introduce new family members gently and look for shared hobbies or interests. If two sides of the blended family have trouble trusting each other, the Libra can encourage them to see each other's good points.

Still, this can be challenging if old resentments exist. The Libra might notice arguments about how to parent or how to handle holidays. Again, the Libra's role as a mediator can be exhausting if they feel stuck between two sides. They may need to learn that while they can encourage fair talks, they cannot force people to get along if they are not ready to find common ground.

Emotional Labor

In some families, one person does most of the "emotional labor," meaning they keep track of everyone's feelings, solve problems, and remember important dates. Libras might find themselves in that role, especially if their calm nature and fairness stand out. They might be the one who calls each relative to check in, who mediates every fight, and who organizes group events that make everyone happy.

While Libras are often good at this, it can be draining if they never get a break. They might want someone else to step in sometimes. If a Libra feels undervalued, they might eventually speak up or become distant. A healthier dynamic is when family members share emotional labor, with each person contributing to making the family a supportive place. Libras might gently suggest dividing responsibilities so they do not feel all the weight on their shoulders.

Caring for Older Relatives

At some point, families might deal with elderly relatives who need extra care. A Libra might approach this with empathy, wanting to ensure the care is shared among siblings or family members. They might say, "We should each take some days to help with meals, errands, and doctor visits, so no one person is overwhelmed." Once again, the Libra aims to split duties in a fair manner.

If they notice one sibling or cousin doing most of the work, they could feel upset about the imbalance. They might try to talk to the rest of the family, hoping they will understand. If the family is unresponsive, the Libra might step up to help, but also feel resentment that others are not pitching in. This situation can test the Libra's ability to set boundaries and assert that fairness is important for everyone's well-being, including their own.

Holiday Conflicts

Holidays can be a joyful time for families, but they can also lead to disputes—where to meet, who cooks, who buys gifts, and so on. A Libra might be the one who tries to plan these events so each branch of the family feels included. They might rotate whose house hosts the event each year, or they might suggest a neutral location so no one feels like their preference is ignored.

If relatives argue about traditions, the Libra might propose a compromise: keep a beloved tradition but also add something fresh that reflects newer family members' ideas. They could say, "Let's do the usual meal, but also let's include a new side dish from your cooking style." This approach tries to respect the old while welcoming the new. Sometimes it works well; other times, certain relatives might resist, which can leave the Libra in the middle once again.

Birth Order Factors

Some families place importance on birth order, with the eldest child getting certain responsibilities and the youngest child being protected. Libras in different birth order positions might experience this differently:

- **Oldest Libra child:** They might have to mediate for younger siblings, try to keep them in line, and show fairness in dividing tasks. They could feel they have extra pressure to be a role model.
- **Middle Libra child:** They might be the classic "bridge" between an older sibling's approach and a younger sibling's needs. They can end up in the peacekeeper role quite often.
- **Youngest Libra child:** They might receive guidance from older siblings but also notice if they are being overprotected. They could try to ensure they are seen as capable and not always treated as the baby of the family.

In all cases, the Libra's desire for fairness can guide how they interact with siblings and parents, shaping family dynamics.

Supporting a Libra in the Family

If you have a Libra in your family, you can support them by recognizing their efforts to keep things balanced. Let them know you appreciate how they mediate or help solve problems. At the same time, try not to rely on them for all emotional labor. Ask how they are doing, or if there is anything you can do to help. This can ease their burden.

Also, encourage them to be honest about their feelings. If you suspect they are holding back frustration or sadness, invite them to open up. A Libra might be relieved to find that sharing concerns does not always lead to yelling or blame. Instead, it can lead to healthier communication that benefits everyone in the family.

Cultural Differences in Families

In families with diverse backgrounds, cultural expectations might collide. For instance, one part of the family could have traditions of strict discipline, while another part favors open discussion. A Libra in the middle might try to help each side understand the other's point of view. They might say, "Let's see if we can merge these approaches," suggesting ways to honor both traditions in a balanced manner.

This can be a real challenge, especially if the cultural differences are large. The Libra may feel anxious if conflicts seem unresolvable. Still, their skill at seeing multiple perspectives can be a big help. If the family is willing to listen, the Libra's calm mediation can create new blends of culture that everyone can enjoy.

Leaving the Nest

When a Libra grows up and moves out of the family home, they might still want to keep a sense of closeness. They may check in with calls or texts, making sure everyone is well. However, if the family tries to control their choices too much, the Libra may set boundaries. They might say, "I love you all, but I need to make some decisions for myself now." This step can be tricky, as Libras do not like conflict, but they also do not want to live under constant control.

Over time, they can find a balanced relationship with their family, where they keep in touch and show care without feeling obligated to live exactly as the family dictates. If tension appears, they will likely try to address it gently, using reason and fairness in their explanations.

Coming Home to Visit

Visits back home can be warm and nostalgic, but they can also bring back old patterns. If the Libra was always the family's peacemaker, they might slip back into that role whether they like it or not. For instance, siblings might start up old arguments, expecting the Libra to calm them down. The Libra could step in automatically or they might try to let the siblings solve it themselves, especially if they have learned to set new limits.

If the Libra has a partner, bringing them to family events might add another layer of dynamics. The Libra will hope their partner and family connect well, but if they do not, the Libra might step in to smooth things over. Once again, they could feel squeezed in the middle. Being mindful of this pattern helps the Libra avoid burnout or over-commitment to playing "referee."

Taking a Stand

One area where Libras might surprise their families is if a big issue of principle arises. For example, if the family expects them to do something deeply unfair or contradictory to the Libra's moral values, the Libra could refuse. While Libras try to please loved ones, they also have a strong sense of right and wrong. If they see a major injustice—like serious mistreatment of a relative or a harmful tradition—they may speak out firmly.

This can catch the family off guard, especially if they are used to the Libra being agreeable. But it is a reminder that fairness does not only mean smoothing things over. Sometimes, it means addressing hard truths. Though the Libra might do it in a measured, polite way, they can stand firm if they believe it is truly necessary.

Emotional Maturity

As Libras mature, they often learn better ways to handle family tensions. They might realize that they cannot fix every conflict, and that sometimes it is okay for people to argue as long as they stay respectful. The Libra could adopt a stance of "I will help if you want me to, but it is not my job to force a solution." This mindset frees them from feeling they must solve every argument.

They might also become more direct in expressing their own feelings, saying things like, "I need a break from this discussion. Let's talk another time," if the conversation becomes too heated. Setting these boundaries can keep them from feeling trapped in the peacemaker role. Over time, family members might respect the Libra's limits, recognizing that calmness does not equal endless patience for everyone else's conflict.

Cherishing Positive Bonds

Despite the challenges, Libras tend to cherish family bonds. If they come from a mostly supportive background, they might speak fondly of the good times, like shared games, group meals, or fun vacations. They might also remember moments when fairness and understanding were shown to them, which in turn helped them grow into caring adults. This sense of appreciation can lead them to maintain close ties with siblings, parents, and other relatives throughout life.

If the family environment was less positive, a Libra might still search for ways to keep at least some ties healthy. They might focus on the relatives who treat them well, limiting contact with those who cause repeated harm. This strategy allows them to keep the family connection while protecting their own well-being.

CHAPTER 9: LIBRA IN THE WORKPLACE

When people talk about Libra traits, they often mention fairness, strong communication skills, and a wish to keep things calm. These qualities can be helpful when Libras enter the workplace. Whether they work in an office, a shop, a school, or any other setting, Libras can stand out for their polite behavior and their ability to bring people together. In this chapter, we will look at how Libras might handle tasks, coworkers, and challenges on the job.

One reason Libras can do well at work is their social nature. Many Libras enjoy talking to others and exchanging ideas. In a job setting, this means a Libra might help different departments or coworkers share information more smoothly. They could bridge communication gaps by calmly listening to everyone's concerns and then clearly explaining the main points to the rest of the team. This can reduce confusion and keep the group focused.

Another strength that Libras bring to the workplace is their sense of fairness. If a group project is assigned, the Libra might check that each member gets an equal chance to contribute. They might say, "Let's divide the tasks in a way that suits everyone's strengths," or "Is there a fair way to handle the workload?" By doing this, the Libra makes sure no one feels ignored or overburdened. This approach can boost team spirit.

Politeness is often a Libra trait that shows up at work. Libras usually mind their words, even if they disagree with someone's approach. They try to avoid heated arguments in front of coworkers, clients, or bosses. This calm style can be reassuring in stressful situations. While some signs might argue loudly about a decision, the Libra tries to keep the discussion respectful. This can help the team stay focused on solving problems rather than fighting.

Libras also tend to be good at building relationships with clients or customers. They might greet people warmly, ask how they are doing, and offer help in a friendly tone. Because they wish to create a calm environment, they might go the extra mile to resolve customer concerns in a fair way. For example, if a customer is upset about a product or service, a Libra might say, "I understand your worries. Let's see how we can fix this so that it feels right for you." This polite and balanced method can help calm tense situations.

In leadership positions, Libras may try to keep harmony among team members. They often lead by cooperation rather than by force. Instead of giving hard commands, they might ask for input: "What do you think is the best approach for this project?" This can help each person on the team feel heard. At the same time, Libras should remember that sometimes a firm decision is needed. If they ask for input all the time without giving direction, the team might feel stuck. So a Libra leader must find a middle path between gathering opinions and setting a clear course of action.

Decision-making can be a tough area for Libras at work, just as it can be in other parts of life. If a Libra manager or employee must choose between two or more options, they might analyze the pros and cons at length. This can be helpful when decisions are complex and need careful thought, but it can cause delays if swift action is required. Coworkers or bosses might say, "We need an answer soon," and a Libra might still be weighing every angle. Over time, Libras can learn to trust their instincts when facts are unclear, or to set deadlines for themselves to avoid overthinking.

Another workplace trait is the Libra's ability to collaborate. They often enjoy the back-and-forth of bouncing ideas off others. A Libra might excel in a job where they can work with teams, lead group discussions, or plan events that involve multiple departments. They may do well in fields like human resources, law, public relations, design, or customer service. These areas let them use their natural talent for smooth communication and fairness. Of course, Libras can work in many fields, but positions that make use of their people skills are often a good match.

Because Libras prefer harmony, they might try to mediate conflicts between coworkers. For instance, if two colleagues are at odds over how to handle a project, a Libra might step in and say, "Let's figure out what each of you wants and see if we can agree on a path." This peacemaking can help the workplace stay calm. On the other hand, Libras should be cautious about taking on the role of constant mediator. If they step in too often, they could tire themselves out or end up in the middle of every conflict. It is important for them to learn that some issues must be solved by the people directly involved.

Libras often notice small details that can improve the work environment. They might see that the break room arrangement feels cramped, so they suggest rearranging tables and chairs to encourage a more open space. Or they might notice that certain rules about fairness are not being followed, such as how schedules or promotions are handled. Because Libras care about even treatment, they could bring these concerns to a supervisor in a calm, polite way. They might say, "I think we can find a more balanced method for scheduling so that no one feels left out."

Another aspect of Libra in the workplace is creativity. If the job involves design, art, or any type of aesthetic focus, Libras might bring fresh ideas. Their sense of balance can show in how they combine colors, layouts, or concepts. Even in roles that are not labeled as creative, Libras might find unique solutions by seeing different sides of a problem. They could say, "We have two approaches; maybe we can merge them to get the best outcome." This is part of the Libra trait of looking for middle ground.

Libras may also pay attention to how they present themselves at work. They often like to look neat or dress in a way that feels balanced and appealing without being too showy. They may choose clothes that match well in color or style, reflecting their interest in things looking orderly. While appearance is not everything, Libras often feel more confident when their outfit is put together in a pleasing way. This can help them make a good impression on clients or managers.

On the flip side, Libras might struggle if the workplace is very chaotic or if people do not respect each other's opinions. In an environment where workers shout or fight, Libras can feel stressed because it goes against their natural wish for peace. They might try to keep calm, but if the environment never improves, they could start to feel anxious or burned out. Libras often do best in a place where colleagues at least aim for respectful discussion, even if they disagree.

When a Libra takes on tasks, they might do better with clear deadlines. If there is no specific end date, they could spend too long polishing their work or pondering small details. Because they strive for a balanced outcome, they might revise again and again to make the project feel just right. This is not always a bad thing, but in fast-paced jobs, they have to know when to wrap up and present their results.

Another factor in Libra's success is feedback. Because Libras value fairness, they usually welcome constructive comments if those comments are given calmly. They might say, "I appreciate the advice.

Let me think about how to use it." However, if a boss or coworker is harsh or insulting, the Libra could take it to heart. They might worry about how to respond without causing conflict. Over time, Libras can practice calmly saying, "I understand you have concerns, but please share them in a respectful way so we can work together to fix the issue."

Libras might also try to befriend coworkers. They can form friendly bonds by chatting about light topics—like weekend plans or shared interests—to create a positive mood. This can help them form a network of allies at work. When a challenge arises, they have people they trust to discuss it with. Coworkers might also like the Libra's balanced approach and ask for help in dealing with workplace friction or planning team events. While being a friendly resource is nice, Libras must watch out for becoming the "office counselor" who never gets their own tasks done.

Managing stress is another area to consider. Many jobs can be high-pressure, especially if deadlines stack up or multiple projects overlap. Libras may try to stay cool under pressure by breaking tasks into smaller steps and seeking help when needed. They might also try to reduce tension by keeping their workspace tidy or adding small touches like a plant or a picture to bring calm. Since Libras like balance, they might set a schedule that includes short breaks to refresh their mind. If the pressure gets too high, though, they might feel overwhelmed and need to talk to a supervisor about adjusting the workload.

In jobs that require negotiations, Libras can excel because they can see both sides of a deal. Whether it is sales, legal work, or even helping team members come to an agreement, the Libra's fair thinking can help them find a solution that feels okay to all parties. They might say, "I hear your main goals, and I also understand the other side's concerns. Let's see if we can strike a balance." This sort of approach can be effective, though it may be slower than a direct, bold negotiation style.

Another positive trait is the Libra's willingness to share credit. If a project succeeds, a Libra will likely say something like, "The whole team did a great job," rather than taking all the praise themselves. This can build goodwill, as coworkers see the Libra as supportive rather than competitive. Of course, Libras also want to be recognized for their efforts. If they are always overlooked, they might feel disappointed. But typically, Libras are happy to spread recognition around.

Libras also pay attention to fairness in promotions or rewards. If they feel a coworker was overlooked despite good performance, they might speak up. They might say to a manager, "This person has worked hard and deserves a chance, too." This can make the Libra a trusted voice for workers who feel unheard. On the flip side, if the Libra themselves is treated unfairly, they might try to address it calmly, showing examples of their work and asking for clear feedback on how they can progress.

Sometimes, Libras may seek roles where they can improve fairness in a broader sense. For instance, they might like human resources jobs, where they can ensure that hiring, training, and pay practices are even for all employees. They might also like roles in social work or nonprofit organizations, where they can help communities or address issues of equity. This aligns with their strong sense of right and wrong. Of course, Libras can succeed in many fields, but these roles might let them feel they are making a difference in terms of balance in the world.

A challenge arises when a Libra must deliver criticism or bad news at work. They might worry about hurting someone's feelings or causing conflict. They could spend a long time finding the right words. While a thoughtful approach is good, if they wait too long, the problem might get worse. Libras can learn to say, "I respect you, but we have to address this issue," in a calm, direct tone. Getting used to occasional conflict as a normal part of workplace life helps them handle these moments better.

Libras may also need to watch out for people who take advantage of their kindness at work. Some coworkers might notice the Libra rarely says no. They could assign extra tasks or leave the Libra to handle difficult clients. Over time, the Libra might feel overwhelmed and wonder why they are doing so much. Learning to say, "I'm sorry, but I have too many tasks right now," can protect them from burnout. A polite but firm refusal can keep them from drowning in extra work.

In group presentations or meetings, Libras can be good at guiding discussion. They might let each person speak, then sum up the points in a neutral way. "So, we have four main ideas here. Let's see if we can combine them." This approach keeps people from talking over each other. Coworkers might appreciate the Libra's calm leadership. However, the Libra must ensure the meeting does not go on too long by always seeking more input. At some point, a conclusion is necessary.

Another skill for Libras is listening. Since they like to be fair, they tend to pay attention when someone describes a problem. This can make them a supportive presence at work, especially for new employees or people who feel nervous. The Libra might mentor or guide a new coworker. They might say, "Let me show you how we handle tasks here. Then you can try, and I'll help if you have questions." This welcoming spirit can build a strong team culture.

Libras might get along well with a boss who respects open communication. If the boss is open to ideas, the Libra will gladly share thoughts on how to make processes smoother. But if the boss is harsh or unfair, the Libra might feel uneasy. They might try to fix the situation through polite requests, but if that fails, they could consider switching to a workplace that matches their values. Libras often hope to find an environment where fairness is at least recognized as a goal, even if things are not perfect.

Managing time is also important. Libras can be thorough, but they risk going overboard in pursuit of a perfectly balanced result. For instance, if they are writing a report, they might check multiple sources, revisit their wording, and try to make the format look nice. If they do not watch the clock, they could miss deadlines. Setting milestones can help. A Libra might say, "I will give myself two hours to gather data, two hours to write, and one hour to review. After that, I'll finalize it no matter what." This system can keep them moving.

Some Libras may thrive in jobs that involve counseling or negotiation. Their ability to weigh different viewpoints calmly can help people in conflict see new solutions. However, this work can also be draining if the Libra absorbs too much tension. They need to practice self-care, maybe stepping away for a quick break or talking to a trusted friend after a stressful mediation. Balancing their emotional well-being is key.

In terms of long-term career growth, Libras might rise to roles where they can shape policies or procedures. For example, if a Libra becomes a manager, they might create guidelines that ensure fair schedules or a clear path for promotions. If they enter a creative field like design or marketing, they might look for projects that let them express their balanced sense of style. They may also gravitate toward roles that involve building bridges—like community outreach or partnership management—since these roles rely on communication and fairness.

A Libra's approach to feedback can also help them climb the career ladder. They usually do not mind hearing ways to improve, as long as it is stated respectfully. If they see a coworker doing something well, they might say, "I really like how you handled that tough client," sharing credit and positivity. This spirit of mutual respect can lead to strong professional bonds over time.

Another point is how Libras cope with office politics. Almost every workplace has some degree of politics, such as people competing for promotions or trying to impress higher-ups. Libras might not enjoy this side of work, since it can involve gossip or pushing others aside. They are likely to stay neutral and focus on fairness, possibly aligning with those who prefer open, honest methods. If pressed to take part in negative politics, a Libra might say, "I'd rather talk about new ideas than talk badly about a coworker," keeping their distance from toxic behavior.

Some Libras might struggle if they want to keep everyone pleased but cannot. For instance, if they supervise a team and must assign tasks that no one wants, someone will inevitably be unhappy. The Libra might feel bad about disappointing a team member. Still, a manager cannot avoid such decisions. In time, Libras learn that fairness does not always mean everyone is fully happy; it can mean giving each person a fair share of both good and challenging tasks.

Libras often do well with group brainstorming. They might organize a session where each person can share an idea without interruption. Then the Libra helps the group find overlaps or ways to merge ideas. This activity suits their skill at balancing opinions. Coworkers might leave the meeting feeling that their voices were heard, which can boost morale. The Libra then helps refine the best points into a workable plan.

For remote or flexible work, Libras might enjoy the independence of managing their own schedule, but they still like to feel connected to the team. They might suggest regular video calls to stay in sync, ensuring no one feels isolated. During those calls, the Libra might check that everyone has a chance to speak, not just the loudest team members. This can make remote work feel more cooperative, reflecting the Libra's wish for inclusive participation.

Conflict resolution is a common theme with Libras. Their ideal workplace is one where people address problems calmly. If they face a colleague who yells or uses rude language, the Libra can feel uncomfortable. They might try to respond in a calm tone, "I hear your concern, but let's talk in a way that helps us solve the issue." If the colleague continues to be rude, the Libra may escalate the matter to a manager. Their main aim is to restore respectful discussion so tasks can proceed.

Recognition is also important for Libras. They like to know that their efforts to maintain harmony, share ideas, or handle tasks have value. If a Libra feels the workplace never acknowledges their input, they might lose motivation. Ideally, a boss or coworker will notice the Libra's unique contributions. A simple "You kept the team on track today—thank you" can encourage a Libra to keep doing what they do best.

Salaries and benefits can also be tied to fairness. Libras might compare what they do with what others do, checking if the pay and rewards line up. If they see big gaps that seem unfair, they might voice their concerns or look for an employer with more balanced policies. Similarly, if they manage a budget for raises, they might try to distribute funds in a way that rewards effort but does not show favoritism.

Over time, Libras can build a reputation at work as someone people can go to for honest and calm advice. They might become a trusted figure for younger staff who need mentoring. However, Libras should remember to look after their own career path too, not just serve others. It is fair for them to say, "I would love to help, but I also need to complete my tasks." This helps them avoid the trap of always putting themselves last.

In summary, Libra in the workplace can be a force for fairness, cooperation, and polite communication. They usually get along well with many types of personalities, as long as everyone tries to act respectfully. The main hurdles they face include decision-making delays, fear of conflict, and the risk of being overburdened by requests for help. By practicing setting boundaries and making timely choices, Libras can thrive. They might excel in roles that draw on their ability to relate to people, solve conflicts, and promote balanced solutions.

Whether they work in a big company or run a small business of their own, Libras can bring a sense of calm, style, and courtesy to their tasks. Their natural wish to treat people well can make the job environment more pleasant for everyone. If they remain aware of their possible weaknesses—such as hesitating too much or avoiding disagreements—they can grow into dependable and respected professionals. Their path at work becomes one of blending thoughtful analysis with timely action, guided by the fairness that is at the heart of the Libra sign.

CHAPTER 10:
DECISION-MAKING AND LIBRA

One of the most well-known traits of Libra is the tendency to weigh choices carefully. While this can lead to balanced judgments, it can also cause delays, confusion, or stress if the Libra hesitates too long. In this chapter, we will look closely at why Libras approach decisions the way they do, how this can be a strength, and what happens when it becomes a stumbling block. We will also explore tips for Libras who want to make decisions more effectively without losing the fairness that defines them.

A big reason Libras are known for careful decision-making is their wish to see all sides of a matter. For example, if they need to pick a new phone, a Libra might compare different brands, models, prices, features, and reviews. They might consider how each option affects their budget, how user-friendly it is, and whether it fits their style. This approach can help them find a phone that truly meets their needs. But if they get stuck trying to find the "perfect" choice, they may never feel ready to settle on one.

In relationships, Libras might weigh small decisions—like choosing a restaurant or selecting a movie—by thinking of what their friend or partner likes, what they themselves like, how far they have to travel, and if anyone has dietary needs or time limits. They do not want to upset the other person, so they might say, "I'm okay with anything. Are you sure you like this plan?" While being considerate, they can also appear indecisive. Over time, they may learn that it is fine to pick a place sometimes. If the other person does not like it, they can speak up.

Another part of Libra's approach is their fondness for compromise. They might say, "Instead of picking one person's idea, can we combine ideas?" This can be a great way to make decisions that honor multiple opinions, but it is not always possible. In some cases, a firm choice is needed, and mixing ideas might water down the result. Libras can become frustrated if they realize there is no perfect compromise. They might feel forced to "pick a side," which can make them anxious.

Many Libras want to avoid conflict. In decision-making, this can mean they hesitate to choose anything that might lead to disagreement. For instance, if a Libra has to decide who gets a certain role in a group project, they may worry that Person A will be upset or Person B will feel overlooked. This can lead to stalling rather than making a direct call. Over time, Libras can discover that no decision will please everyone all the time, and that some level of disagreement might be normal.

On the bright side, Libra's balanced view can be a big advantage when decisions are complex. Suppose a team at work needs to pick between two strategies, each with pros and cons. The Libra might lay out the facts in a clear, unbiased way: "Strategy 1 costs less but might take longer to see results. Strategy 2 is faster but more expensive. Which is best for our goals?" By presenting both sides evenly, the Libra helps the group see the bigger picture. This can lead to thoughtful and fair decisions.

Libras often try to make decisions that feel morally correct. They might ask, "Is this good for everyone involved?" or "Is anyone harmed by this choice?" This sense of ethics can guide them to stand up for what they believe is right. For instance, if a Libra must decide whether to speak up about an unfair policy, they might weigh the risk of causing tension against the benefit of promoting fairness.

Ultimately, many Libras decide that fighting for what is just is worth the discomfort.

However, the quest for moral balance can become tiring if the Libra feels responsible for every outcome. Some choices do not have huge moral weight—like which color to paint a room or what flavor of ice cream to try—but Libras might still worry about letting people down. They might ask everyone's opinion, hoping for a consensus, even on small matters. This can slow down the process. Learning which decisions need broad input and which do not is a key skill for Libras.

A Libra might also face analysis paralysis, a term used when a person cannot decide because they have too many factors in mind. They might research a topic for hours, gather information from various sources, and then find themselves overwhelmed by details. This can happen with important life choices, like picking a college major, a job, or a city to live in. Libras can become stuck if they wait for perfect clarity. In reality, no path is guaranteed to be perfect, and they might need to trust their own instincts at some point.

Another factor is that Libras often want to be liked. They might fear that a strong choice could make some people dislike them. For example, if they have to choose who joins a club or team, they might be afraid of rejecting one candidate. They know that person might take it personally. But as they grow, Libras learn that decisions sometimes carry disappointments. They can still be gentle in how they share the outcome, but they cannot avoid all negative reactions.

When faced with a decision, Libras might list pros and cons. This is a common tactic that can help them see the situation clearly. They might write down what they stand to gain or lose and what others might gain or lose. Once they compare lists, they can pick the side with the most benefits or fewest drawbacks. However, if both sides appear equal, Libras might end up back at square one. They may need to factor in personal gut feelings or ask for advice from someone they trust.

Seeking input from trusted friends can help a Libra make decisions. They might say, "I have these two options. Which do you think fits me better?" A friend might remind them of past situations or personal goals that the Libra forgot to consider. Still, Libras must be sure not to ask too many people. If they gather five opinions and each person says something different, the Libra could get even more confused. Limiting feedback to a few respected voices can be more helpful

Sometimes, Libras might delay making a choice until circumstances force their hand. For example, if they are picking a class to take, they might wait until the last day to sign up because they cannot decide. Then they discover only one class still has openings. This can lead to a rushed or random decision. While it might work out, Libras often feel uneasy about letting events choose for them. Practicing earlier action can give them a sense of control

In romantic relationships, decision-making can be a delicate area. A Libra might struggle to pick a wedding venue or a style for the home they share with their partner. They want the partner's input, but they also might have their own ideas. They do not want to appear bossy, yet they do not want to be a doormat either. This balancing act can be exhausting if they overthink every detail. Talking openly with the partner about dividing decision-making tasks can help. For instance, the partner might choose the food menu while the Libra focuses on decorations.

When Libras do make a choice, they often strive to carry it out with grace. If they have to give bad news—like telling a person they did not get a position—they try to phrase it kindly. If they pick an approach in a group setting, they try to explain their reasoning so people understand it was a fair choice. This method can reduce hurt feelings, though it takes more time than simply saying "No" or "Yes." Libras see it as worth the effort if it keeps peace and clarity.

A hidden strength in Libra decision-making is their ability to adapt if they see a better solution. For instance, if a Libra chooses a certain path but then new information appears, they can revisit the decision. They might say, "It turns out we have a better option now. Let's reconsider." While some see this as flip-flopping, it can also be a sign of flexibility. The key is not to switch back and forth so often that nobody knows what is going on. Libras can keep reevaluation to times when it truly matters.

Some Libras find it helpful to set deadlines for themselves. They might say, "I will give myself three days to research, then I must decide." This puts a clear stop to endless pondering. If they still feel unsure after the research period, they can rely on their best judgment. They might also remind themselves that many decisions are not permanent. If they pick a new hobby and do not like it, they can try another. Giving themselves permission to correct course later can ease the pressure to find the one perfect answer.

Another strategy is to check which values matter most to them in a given choice. For example, if the main value is saving money, they can give more weight to cost factors. If the main value is learning new things, they can focus on which option teaches them more. By ranking their values ahead of time, Libras can break a tie when the facts look similar. This helps them prioritize what matters instead of getting stuck in an equal balance.

Libras may also talk about their worries out loud to clarify their thoughts. Sometimes hearing themselves explain the issue helps them realize which direction feels right. They could do this with a friend or even alone, speaking into a recorder or writing in a journal. The act of putting feelings into words can highlight hidden preferences. They might say, "I keep talking about how Option B excites me. Maybe that is a sign."

In workplaces, Libras must strike a balance between gathering opinions and taking initiative. If they invite too many viewpoints, the team can run in circles. The Libra might practice saying, "Thank you for the input. I will use it to make a decision by Friday." This ensures everyone feels heard but also sets a firm endpoint. Coworkers will trust the Libra's process if they see that it leads to real action rather than endless debate.

In personal life, big decisions like moving to a new city, buying a home, or changing careers can overwhelm a Libra if they do not break it down. They might list steps: research locations, compare costs, check job options, then pick the top two and visit them if possible. Each step has its own mini-decision, which can feel less daunting than one giant leap. This method helps the Libra stay calm and methodical.

Over time, Libras learn that not every decision is equally important. Some choices—like which socks to wear—can be made quickly without harm. Others—like which car to buy—require more thought. By learning to gauge the impact of a decision, they can focus their energy on the choices that really matter. This helps them avoid feeling worn out from overthinking small things.

Another key lesson for Libras is that making no choice can be worse than picking imperfectly. Life often rewards decisive action, even if mistakes happen. For example, if they wait too long to accept a job offer, the company might give it to someone else. Then the Libra ends up with no job at all. Realizing that a "good enough" choice is better than none can push them to act earlier.

Libras also benefit from seeing that disagreements are not always bad. Friends or coworkers might actually respect someone who takes a stance, even if they do not agree. Standing up for a position can show strength of character. As long as the Libra remains polite, others often accept that they cannot get everything their way. By stepping into minor conflicts when necessary, Libras can avoid bigger, hidden tensions that come from never addressing issues.

Once a decision is made, Libras may second-guess themselves. They could think, "What if the other option was better?" This sense of regret or doubt can linger if they do not trust their own process. A helpful approach is to remind themselves why they chose what they did. They might keep a short note: "I picked Option A because it fit my budget and aligned with my schedule." Reading it can ease the fear of missing out on the other path.

Libras can also learn from any decision that turns out poorly. Instead of blaming themselves for being bad at choosing, they can analyze what went wrong. Was there a piece of information they missed? Did they rely too much on someone else's advice? Did they ignore a strong gut feeling? By looking at the issue calmly, they gain wisdom for future choices.

Sometimes, Libras do best if they start with a smaller range of options. Having too many choices—like 50 different car models—can lead to confusion. They might narrow it down quickly: "I want a car that is fuel-efficient, reliable, and within this price range." That might cut the list to five or six models, making the final selection more manageable. This is a way of pre-sorting options based on known deal-breakers.

Another piece of advice for Libras is to set a personal standard for how much research is enough. If they tend to read every blog or review, they might decide in advance, "I will consult three trusted sources, then decide." This keeps them from endless searching. They can also add a time limit: "I will spend two days gathering facts, then

I will pick." Having these rules in place can curb the urge to keep looking for new opinions.

In team settings, Libras might delegate parts of the decision to others. For instance, if a Libra is leading an event planning committee, they might assign one person to pick the food, another to pick the location, and so on. The Libra oversees fairness but does not personally weigh every tiny detail. This method allows them to focus on the bigger picture while trusting others to handle their assigned tasks. It also teaches Libras that sharing control can free them from the full weight of decisions.

Libras also can reflect on their successes. When they make a choice that turns out well, they might keep a mental note of it. Remembering positive outcomes can remind them that they are capable of making good calls. Too often, people recall mistakes more clearly than wins, which can feed anxiety. By focusing on their own track record of thoughtful decisions, Libras can build confidence.

Sometimes, letting go of the idea that a choice has to be ideal can help. Libras might say, "I'll aim for a choice that seems balanced, but it may not be perfect." This realistic view lowers the stress of finding a flawless option. They can also remember that if a problem arises, they are creative enough to adapt. This thought encourages them to pick something rather than stay stuck.

Libras can also practice small decisions daily as a form of training. For example, they can decide quickly what to eat for breakfast or what route to take to school or work, without overthinking. By exercising their "decision muscle" on minor things, they learn to trust themselves more. Over time, this skill can carry over into bigger choices.

When dealing with family or close friends, Libras might fear hurting loved ones by making certain decisions. They can help by sharing reasons in a gentle but direct way. For instance, "I know you want me to live nearby, but I took a job offer far away because it can help me grow in my career." A calm explanation can ease tensions, and while it might not erase disappointment, it shows respect. Libras can then move forward knowing they handled it with kindness.

If a Libra still feels overwhelmed, talking to a counselor or coach might be a good idea. Professionals can offer tools for decision-making. They might have exercises that help a Libra pinpoint core values or weigh options more quickly. This outside perspective can also break old habits of hesitation. The goal is not to turn Libras into impulsive decision-makers, but to help them find a comfortable level of certainty.

As Libras get older, many grow more confident about what they truly want. They might be less swayed by outside opinions or the fear of conflict. They realize that fairness does not always require waiting for everyone's approval. Some choices must be made for personal well-being or life progress. This self-assurance can reduce the anxiety that once accompanied every decision.

Decision-making for Libras remains a blend of logic, empathy, and a hope that outcomes work well for everyone. When balanced, this approach leads to thoughtful and ethical choices. When taken too far, it can cause indecision or a habit of people-pleasing. Libras who accept that some choices will always make a few people unhappy can feel freer to follow their own guidance. They can hold onto the best parts of their balanced style without letting the process become an endless loop.

In summary, Libras take decision-making seriously because they value fairness, harmony, and shared happiness. They gather details, consider how others feel, and try to avoid causing upset. This can lead to wise actions when they manage it well. But it can also lead to overthinking if they fear making mistakes or sparking conflict. By learning practical methods—like setting deadlines, limiting input, focusing on key values, and accepting that not all outcomes can be ideal—Libras can handle choices with more ease. This growth helps them remain true to their balanced nature while also being timely and confident.

At its heart, Libra's approach to decisions reflects their wish to respect everyone involved. This is a kind trait, especially in a world that can sometimes be rushed or harsh. Yet, Libras can remember that they themselves are part of "everyone." Their own needs and feelings are as important as others' wishes. Including their own voice in the balance will help them make choices that feel fair not just to others, but to themselves as well.

Ultimately, decision-making does not have to be a constant struggle for Libras. With practice, they can become experts at spotting the key factors, weighing them calmly, and deciding in a way that respects their sense of right and wrong. They can also realize that being decisive and being fair are not opposites. When Libras reach this understanding, they often find that their decisions become an expression of both their caring heart and their wise mind.

As with many facets of life, it all comes down to balance. Libras naturally look for that balance in choices big and small. By trusting their own reasoning, seeking input wisely, and accepting that no choice is flawless, they can make decisions that reflect both logic and kindness. This is the essence of how Libras handle decision-making: aiming for the fairest path, but also knowing they can move forward without worrying that they must please everyone perfectly every single time.

CHAPTER 11: THE EMOTIONAL LIFE OF LIBRA

People often talk about Libra's calm and balanced side, but behind that calm image is a range of emotions that can be deep and complex. Libras want to feel happy and at peace, yet they also experience worries, sadness, and excitement like anyone else. In this chapter, we will look at how Libras handle these feelings, how they express them, and what challenges they might face when their emotions become strong.

A common thought is that Libras aim for emotional balance. They like situations that feel peaceful, so they try to keep their feelings under steady control. This does not mean Libras do not feel strong emotions. It simply means they prefer calm ways of dealing with them. If a Libra is upset, they might take a deep breath and wait before speaking. They hope to avoid saying harsh things in the heat of the moment. This approach can be helpful but may lead to bottling up emotions if they wait too long to share them.

Libras often have a strong desire to keep everyone around them happy. This might include parents, friends, coworkers, or romantic partners. Because of this, they might ignore their own feelings to focus on others' needs. For instance, if a friend is sad, a Libra may place their own worries aside to offer support. This can show kindness, but it can also leave the Libra feeling unseen if no one asks about their own stress or sadness.

Another aspect of Libra's emotional life is sensitivity to conflict. Libras tend to avoid harsh fights or loud arguments. When the mood around them is tense, they might feel uneasy. They could try to make peace or lighten the atmosphere with a gentle remark. If that fails, they might withdraw and hope the tension fades on its own. Over time, they might learn that some conflicts need direct attention. Ignoring them can lead to bigger problems later.

Libras also have a notable sense of empathy. They often notice how other people feel. If someone is down, a Libra might pick up on their body language or the tone of their voice. They might say, "Are you okay? You seem worried," offering a listening ear. This empathy can help them form strong friendships, as people appreciate feeling understood. However, absorbing others' feelings can weigh heavily on a Libra's heart, especially if they already have their own troubles.

When it comes to positive emotions like excitement or joy, Libras might express these in a modest way. They are usually not the type to jump around shouting. Instead, a Libra might show happiness with a warm smile, a small laugh, or a gentle cheer. Yet, inside, they can feel very pleased. Some Libras do share bigger outward signs of happiness, but many prefer a calmer style of expression. They want to remain polite and thoughtful of those around them.

Romantic feelings can bring a swirl of emotions for Libras. They might feel deep affection for someone, but they can be cautious about showing it too quickly, fearing rejection or conflict. They might show small acts of care—like remembering a loved one's favorite snack or writing a kind note—rather than dramatic displays. At times, a Libra might worry that their gentle style goes unnoticed if the other person expects grand gestures. Learning to speak openly about affection can help Libras feel more at ease in love.

In family settings, Libras can be the ones who check on everyone's emotions. They might notice if a sibling looks sad or if a parent is stressed. Then they might try to offer help. If the family is loud or prone to arguments, a Libra could feel overwhelmed. They might step out of the room until calm returns or try to talk gently with each side. While this can keep harmony, it can also leave the Libra worn out if they constantly manage other people's tempers.

Stress is another emotional factor for Libras. They can feel stressed when deadlines loom or when multiple responsibilities pile up. Because they want things to be fair and nicely handled, they might spend extra time planning or worrying. If they cannot find a balanced approach, they might feel anxious. Some Libras manage stress by seeking quiet hobbies, such as reading, painting, or taking nature walks. These activities can help them clear their mind. If they do not find a way to release tension, they might become moody or irritable.

Anger can be tricky for Libras. They usually do not like feeling angry, because it disrupts their sense of harmony. If something truly upsets them, they might hold it in at first. Over time, the anger could build until they finally speak out in frustration. This can surprise the people around them, who thought the Libra was unaffected. A healthier path is for Libras to learn to say, "That bothers me," as soon as they notice it. Speaking calmly but directly can prevent bottled-up anger from bursting out in an unpleasant way.

Guilt is another emotion that might affect Libras. Because they aim to please, they could feel guilty when they have to say no or put their own needs first. For example, if a friend asks for help but the Libra is already busy, the Libra might still feel bad about refusing. To handle this, Libras can remind themselves that they deserve rest and space. Being fair means being fair to themselves, too. Overcoming unnecessary guilt can help them set healthier boundaries.

Libras also experience delight when they see that their actions have made someone's day better. If they share a kind word or a helpful deed, and the other person smiles or says thanks, the Libra feels warm inside. They might think, "I helped create a peaceful moment."

This positive feeling can encourage them to keep being kind. The challenge arises if they rely on that praise or gratitude to feel okay about themselves. Learning self-worth from within, rather than always from others' feedback, can strengthen a Libra's emotional well-being.

Sometimes, Libras can struggle with envy or jealousy, especially if they see others receiving praise they hoped for. However, because they like to stay polite, they might hide such feelings behind a pleasant face. If these feelings get strong, they might quietly become distant or unhappy. The best solution is to admit, at least to themselves, "I feel jealous right now," and ask why. Often, it is because they think the other person has an advantage or is receiving unfair favor. Once they see the root cause, they can address it more calmly.

Another key point is how Libras handle sadness. When they feel low, they might isolate themselves or put on a brave smile so no one sees the pain. They might worry about burdening others with their sadness or making the mood heavy. If they do not open up to someone they trust, the sadness can linger longer than it needs to. Finding a safe place to share—like a close friend, a family member, or even a counselor—can help Libras process their sorrow. Talking about it does not mean they are weak; it can actually show healthy self-awareness.

Libras may use their creativity to handle strong emotions. For instance, they might write poems or keep a journal to sort out their feelings. Others might turn to art or music as an outlet for what they cannot easily say out loud. These forms of expression let a Libra release sadness, anger, or happiness in a constructive way. By channeling emotions into something meaningful, they can maintain a sense of calm on the outside while still exploring their deeper feelings.

Humor is another tool Libras might use to lighten heavy emotions. If they sense tension in a room, they might make a gentle joke or share a funny story. This can ease the mood and help everyone relax. But Libras should watch out that they do not use humor to avoid serious issues that need discussion. A balanced approach is to add a bit of lightness when appropriate but also face real problems directly.

A big emotional test for Libras is learning to say "I can't do that" or "I need help." They might fear that asking for help will trouble someone, or that refusing a request will create bad feelings. Yet, to protect their own emotional health, they must accept that it is not possible to help everyone or handle every job alone. By communicating their limits, Libras can prevent burnout and lessen resentment that builds up from doing too much.

Another emotional pattern can appear when Libras are forced to pick sides in a conflict. They might feel torn if two friends or family members are at odds. The Libra's natural reaction is to see both points of view, which can leave them unsure of how to proceed. They might attempt to make each side see reason or find a middle ground. Emotionally, this can be draining, as they fear hurting either friend. Accepting that they cannot always fix other people's conflicts can help them manage the stress.

Libras also like feelings of appreciation and acceptance. They might put in extra effort at work or in friendships hoping to be thanked or recognized. While wanting acknowledgment is normal, relying too much on outside approval can lead to emotional ups and downs. If praise is given, they feel wonderful; if it is withheld, they feel disappointed. Learning to value themselves based on personal effort and growth, rather than external applause, can create a steadier emotional base.

Coping with failure can be hard for some Libras, especially if they see it as letting others down. If they do not achieve a desired goal, they might dwell on what went wrong, feeling regret. They could ask themselves, "Did I make the right choices? Did I consider everyone's needs?" If they remain stuck in this loop, it can harm their confidence. A healthier way is to take a balanced view: see what they can learn from the failure without turning it into an overwhelming emotional burden.

A Libra's emotional life also shapes how they spend free time. Because they seek calm, they might choose relaxed activities, such as quiet gatherings with friends, art projects, or reading. If they go to a large event or a loud place, they might enjoy it for a while but could feel drained afterward. They might need time alone or with a close friend to process the extra stimulation. Knowing their own emotional limits can help Libras plan their schedules in a way that keeps them balanced.

When faced with big life changes—like moving to a new place, changing schools, or starting a different job—Libras may feel both excitement and worry. On one hand, they like the idea of new experiences. On the other, they fret about whether they will fit in or if the change will upset their established peace. Emotions can swirl as they weigh the pros and cons. During these times, a Libra might lean on close friends or family for comfort and advice. They might also make lists of what they find positive versus what worries them, trying to restore emotional balance.

Libras might deal with heartbreak more gently than some signs, choosing quiet reflection or talking to a few close people instead of making it a big scene. They might blame themselves if they think they were unfair or did not consider the other person's viewpoint enough. Or, if they feel the other person wronged them, they might struggle with lingering questions about how to maintain polite communication moving forward. It can help them to remember that heartbreak is often nobody's fault, and that it is a normal part of human relationships.

Anxiety can creep up when Libras see too many possible outcomes for a situation. They can feel restless if they do not know which direction an event is headed. They may try to soothe themselves by seeking more information or talking it out with a friend. In some cases, a Libra might need to simply accept uncertainty. Learning that not everything can be fully predicted or controlled can ease the emotional strain. Breathing exercises or simple relaxation techniques can also bring calm in moments of worry.

A personal challenge for Libras is to avoid letting fear of conflict freeze them emotionally. Sometimes they might know they are unhappy with a situation, but they keep smiling to avoid making waves. This can lead to an inner build-up of stress, which might burst out later in tears or sudden anger. Practicing small steps of honesty—such as saying, "I felt uncomfortable about what happened earlier"—can help them handle conflict in a healthier, more direct manner.

Libras sometimes show compassion by volunteering or helping charities. Their concern for fairness might drive them to support groups that aid people or animals in need. This can bring them emotional satisfaction as they see their time and effort making a difference. They might form emotional bonds with those they help, feeling each success or setback deeply. They do need to watch out for compassion fatigue, which happens if they give more than they can handle. Setting boundaries keeps them from burning out while still being supportive.

Another emotional pattern in Libras is the tendency to smooth over differences. If they meet someone with a very different view, they might try to find shared ground quickly, so no one feels tension. While this can create pleasant interactions, Libras might feel frustrated if they stifle their own beliefs too often. Balancing politeness with authenticity helps them stay true to themselves while still being respectful of others.

When Libras do feel upset or depressed, they might want to retreat to a calm, private spot. They might take a walk outside, spend time in a quiet room, or listen to gentle music. These methods let them process feelings without external pressure. If their sadness persists, they may reach out to one trusted friend rather than many acquaintances. They prefer a soothing, private talk over big group discussions of their problems.

Libras can benefit from regular check-ins with their own feelings. They might keep a short daily log: "Today I felt stressed about a project, but I talked with my coworker, and we found a plan. I still feel some worry, but it's less." By tracking these day-to-day emotions, they learn patterns—like triggers that cause the most upset or methods that help them calm down. Over time, they can develop healthy habits for managing emotional swings.

Some Libras enjoy uplifting others through acts of kindness or compliments. Telling a coworker, "Your idea was really helpful," or giving a friend a small gift can boost the Libra's own mood, too, because they see a positive reaction. However, they must make sure they are not ignoring their own needs just to keep others feeling good. Self-care is vital for Libras, even if they feel guilty focusing on themselves at first.

Another point is that Libras appreciate beauty, which can soothe their emotions. This might involve decorating their room with pleasant colors or putting fresh flowers on the table. It can also mean visiting art galleries, attending small concerts, or simply observing nature. These peaceful sights and sounds help them relax. When they are stressed or sad, seeking beauty around them might serve as a gentle remedy.

Overthinking is a habit that can tie in with Libra emotions. They might replay a conversation in their head, wondering if they offended someone or if they seemed rude. They could worry about possible misunderstandings. If this happens too often, it can lead to mental fatigue. One way to break the loop is to ask for clarification—"I hope I didn't upset you earlier"—or simply realize that minor missteps happen in any relationship. Accepting imperfection can bring emotional relief.

As Libras grow older, many learn to be more direct about their feelings. They discover that gentle honesty often leads to better understanding than silence or constant politeness. With time, they see that speaking up early prevents bigger emotional turmoil later. They may still prefer a calm tone, but they do not shy away from saying, "I feel frustrated right now. Let's talk about it."

Stressful events—like losing a job, facing a health issue, or dealing with heartbreak—can test a Libra's usual emotional balance. At first, they might feel overwhelmed or more anxious than usual. However, their strong desire for harmony can motivate them to find ways to cope. They might reach out for support, set up a plan to handle the problem, and remind themselves that they have overcome challenges before. Each test can teach them new lessons about handling strong emotions.

Another helpful step for Libras is accepting that life has ups and downs. Trying to keep emotions smooth all the time is impossible. Some days will bring conflict, and some will bring surprises. By preparing mentally for these shifts, Libras can remain calmer when trouble hits. They might say, "I can't avoid feeling sad sometimes, but I can choose how I respond." This mindset helps them adapt without feeling that every negative emotion is a failure.

Building emotional resilience includes discovering which people in their life truly support them. Libras may have many acquaintances but only a few close friends who understand their deeper struggles. Keeping these close connections strong allows a Libra to express real feelings without fear of being judged. In return, they can also offer empathy, creating a balanced bond of sharing and listening.

A Libra's emotional world can be full of complexity, yet also guided by the aim of kindness. They often want to be fair to others' feelings while preserving their own sense of calm. Their strengths include empathy, diplomacy, and a desire to see the best in people. Their struggles may involve fear of conflict, indecision, and bottling up anger or sadness. By understanding these patterns, Libras can handle emotional turbulence more smoothly.

Relaxation methods can help Libras stay on top of strong feelings. This might include easy breathing exercises, short meditation sessions, or simple stretches. Even taking five minutes to breathe quietly can lower stress levels. Libras might also enjoy journaling, describing how they feel about certain events and noting any improvements. Over time, these habits can form a safety net that catches them before emotions become overwhelming.

In sum, the emotional life of Libra is shaped by the wish to keep things calm and fair while still experiencing the full range of human feelings. They can face worries about conflict, guilt when refusing others, or stress over making everyone happy. Yet, they can also find great joy in helping friends, appreciating beauty, and forming strong, thoughtful bonds. By learning to speak up when emotions run high, and by balancing their own needs with their care for others, Libras can maintain a healthy emotional life that reflects the true harmony they aim for in all areas.

Ultimately, Libras grow the most when they realize that their own well-being is just as important as the peace they try to create for others. Emotions are a normal part of human life, and it is good to explore them. With patience, support, and honest communication, Libras can honor their feelings and still remain the gentle, fair-minded souls who bring calm to the people around them.

CHAPTER 12: LIBRA AND COMMUNICATION

Communication is a big part of how Libras connect with others. Many people say Libras have a special way with words, aiming to be kind and balanced when they speak. They often choose phrases that do not sound harsh or dismissive. This chapter will focus on how Libras communicate, how they listen, and what challenges they might face in conversations. We will also look at ways Libras can keep communication open and clear without losing their gentle approach.

A key feature of Libra-style communication is politeness. Libras usually do not like rude or aggressive language. If they sense the tone of a conversation getting tense, they might try to soften it with calmer words. For example, instead of saying "You are wrong," they might say, "I see your point, but have we thought about this other angle?" This approach can lower the chance of heated arguments.

Libras often practice active listening. They look people in the eye, nod to show they are following along, and ask clarifying questions like, "Do you mean this?" or "Could you tell me more about that?" This signals genuine interest and helps avoid misunderstandings. Because they want fairness, they might make sure everyone has a turn to speak in a group setting. However, if the group is large or some people talk a lot, a Libra might have to step in and gently guide the conversation, saying something like, "Let's hear from those who haven't spoken yet."

Another part of Libra's communication style is seeking agreement or common ground. Even if they disagree with someone, they might say, "I understand why you feel that way," before sharing their own view. This can help build a bridge between different opinions. By showing empathy first, Libras reduce resistance and keep the talk respectful. However, it can be a problem if the Libra overemphasizes the other person's view at the expense of their own. A balance is needed.

Because Libras want harmony, they might avoid topics they think will spark conflict, such as deep disagreements on personal beliefs. If a coworker or a family member tries to engage in a heated debate, the Libra might steer the discussion toward safer ground. Sometimes this is helpful, but other times important issues need to be discussed. Libras can learn to address such issues calmly rather than ignoring them. This way, they respect the need for open communication while still keeping a civil tone.

In friendships, Libras often use caring words. They might send small messages to friends, like "Hope you're doing well" or "Thinking of you." This shows that they value the friendship and want to maintain a sense of connection. They might also be the friend who organizes a group call or chat, making sure everyone can update each other. Because they like fairness, they will try to prevent one friend from monopolizing the conversation.

At work, Libras can excel at teamwork because of their communication. They might gather each coworker's thoughts, then present a summary that blends the best ideas. They do this in a respectful way, giving credit to each person. Colleagues might appreciate how the Libra keeps talks flowing. A risk is that if two coworkers strongly oppose each other, the Libra could get stuck in the role of peacemaker. If this happens too often, it can be draining.

Knowing when to mediate and when to let others solve their own conflicts is important.

In romantic situations, Libras often prefer polite, affectionate talk. They might enjoy gentle flirting, using compliments that show genuine notice of the other person's qualities. For instance, a Libra might say, "I really like how you always see the bright side" or "You have a calming presence." These soft words help create a warm atmosphere. However, if something is bothering them, a Libra might hesitate to mention it for fear of spoiling the mood. Over time, unspoken issues can become big. Being direct can prevent misunderstandings in love.

Social media can be another channel for Libra communication. They might share posts or images that reflect positivity and balance, or add calm comments to friends' updates. If an online argument starts in the comments, a Libra might try to calm it by adding a measured viewpoint. If the argument is too hot, they might simply leave the conversation, not wanting to get caught in a storm of negativity.

Tone of voice is something Libras watch closely. They might speak in a moderate volume, not too loud, to avoid sounding pushy. They might also use a friendly or gentle pitch to show they are not threatening or angry. This can help in tense situations, since it signals that the Libra is willing to talk calmly. On the other hand, if a Libra's voice is always soft, some people might not take them seriously. Libras can learn to speak with more firmness when they need to be heard clearly.

Body language also matters. Libras might stand or sit in a relaxed, open posture when talking. They could tilt their head or lean in slightly to show interest. If the other person crosses their arms or looks away, the Libra might read that as discomfort or disagreement. Then they might ask, "Is something on your mind?" This attempt to check the other person's feelings often builds trust, but it can be a lot of emotional work if the Libra does it constantly.

When faced with criticism, Libras try to respond politely rather than become defensive right away. They might say, "Thank you for telling me that. I'll think about how to improve." However, if the criticism is delivered in a rude way, Libras might feel hurt or uncertain about how to reply. They may try to calm the situation by suggesting a more respectful tone, or they might quietly walk away to prevent a scene. Over time, Libras can learn that being direct—"I hear your feedback, but could we discuss it more kindly?"—is better than letting rude comments go unaddressed.

Another communication challenge is confrontation. Because Libras dislike conflict, they sometimes wait too long to address serious problems. For instance, if a roommate keeps making a mess, a Libra might drop hints instead of speaking plainly: "I'm having trouble keeping the kitchen clean. Maybe we should all pitch in more." The roommate might not realize how upset the Libra truly is. Eventually, the Libra might burst out in frustration, which seems out of nowhere. Learning to say, "I need to talk about this problem" at an earlier stage can save them from stored-up anger.

Libras also value politeness in written communication, like emails or letters. They typically use greetings and closings, such as "Hello, hope you're doing well" and "Thank you for your time." This helps set a friendly tone. They might carefully choose words so they do not come across as harsh. If they need to say something negative, they might sandwich it between positive statements, like "I appreciate your effort, but we need to adjust this part. I know we can find a good solution."

When they feel strongly about an issue, Libras might still present their view in a careful way. For example, if they think a rule at school or work is unfair, they could gather facts first and then say, "I've noticed that this rule affects some people more than others. Could we reconsider it?" This calm approach can be persuasive, though some people might wish the Libra showed more passion. Balancing calmness with earnest conviction can help Libras be effective advocates for fairness.

In group discussions, Libras often act as moderators. If two people are talking at once, the Libra might gently say, "Let's let them finish, then we'll hear your point." This role can keep the conversation organized, but it also places pressure on the Libra to remain neutral. Sometimes they do have their own opinions, which they might hold back so the group does not feel they are taking sides. Over time, Libras can learn to moderate while still sharing their personal stance.

When talking to children, Libras might use a gentle, encouraging tone. They believe in explaining the "why" behind rules. For example, "We don't push each other because it can hurt feelings, and we want everyone to feel safe." This helps children understand the reasons for polite behavior, rather than just obeying out of fear. Libras might also invite questions from kids, patiently answering them so the child feels respected.

If a Libra finds themselves in a leadership role, they might hold open forums or Q&A sessions to gather input from the group. Their goal is to ensure everyone's voice is heard. This can make team members feel valued, but the Libra must also be prepared to make a final call if opinions conflict. Communication in leadership for a Libra means merging fairness with decisiveness. Otherwise, people might say the Libra never sets a clear direction.

In a crisis, Libras might try to keep the tone calm so that people do not panic. They could say, "Let's focus on the steps we need to take right now." However, if the situation is truly urgent, a Libra might need to speak more firmly and quickly than usual. Their natural mildness could be mistaken for a lack of seriousness. Practicing a clear, strong voice for emergencies can help them lead effectively when needed.

Libras often pay attention to word choice. They may avoid words that sound too harsh, like "hate" or "never." Instead, they might say, "It bothers me when this happens" or "I rarely agree with that idea." This subtle difference can soften the impact of disagreement. But if a Libra is too careful, they might not convey the real urgency of a matter. Learning to adjust word choice based on the situation is a skill they can develop.

When a Libra needs to set a boundary, their communication might include polite disclaimers: "I value our friendship, but I need some space today." This helps them feel they are not being rude. It also shows the other person that the Libra still cares about the relationship. However, if a boundary is critical—like stopping someone from overstepping personal limits—the Libra might need to be more direct: "I need you to understand that this can't happen anymore."

Online chats can sometimes cause misunderstandings because the tone is not clear. Libras might use emojis or gentle phrasing to show friendliness. If a friend or coworker writes back in a blunt way, the Libra might wonder if they did something wrong. They could ask for a quick call or an in-person chat to clear things up. Knowing that online messages can sound colder than intended can help Libras avoid taking them too personally.

Libras may also enjoy talking about topics that involve comparing ideas, like reviews of books, art, or music. Their balanced nature can help them see the good points in different styles or opinions. They might say, "I appreciate this artist for their creativity, but I also like how the other artist focuses on simple designs." This even-handed approach can spark interesting discussions where no one feels attacked for liking something else.

Humor can be part of Libra communication, though it is often a light touch rather than a sharp wit. They might share a funny observation or a gentle pun that eases tension. If a conversation is getting too heavy, a Libra might drop in a small joke to remind everyone to stay relaxed. However, they typically avoid humor that mocks or belittles others, as that goes against their sense of kindness.

Communication style can change depending on the audience. If Libras are with very close friends, they might be more open and playful. If they are with strangers or in a formal setting, they might keep their tone polite and neutral, focusing on friendly small talk rather than personal stories. This adaptation helps them navigate different social circles, but can leave them feeling tired if they must constantly adjust to please many groups.

In times of grief or sadness, Libras might find it hard to express their own pain. They might speak softly about their feelings or avoid the topic altogether, fearing it could burden others. Yet, when a friend is sad, Libras usually offer comforting words and listen patiently. They might say, "I'm here for you," or "I wish I could take away your pain." This gentle reassurance can mean a lot to someone who is hurting.

Libras might have a knack for writing well-structured essays, letters, or articles. Their sense of balance can show in how they organize ideas in a logical sequence. They might start with a friendly introduction, present both sides of a topic, and then conclude with a fair summary. This can make them good at tasks that involve explaining information clearly, such as instructional materials or policy briefs.

One tricky spot is when Libras must deliver bad news. They might write a polite message that circles around the point, hoping to soften the blow. For example, "Thank you for applying. We liked many parts of your proposal, but sadly we can't move forward at this time." While this is kinder than a blunt rejection, it can also leave the other person wondering if there is more to the story. Libras can improve by giving a brief, honest reason, helping the other side understand the situation fully.

Another point is that Libras sometimes speak slowly when they are thinking carefully about each word. This can show thoughtfulness, but in a fast-paced environment, people might interrupt them or finish their sentences. Libras can practice speaking more briskly or telling others, "I need a moment to finish my thought," so they are not talked over. Standing firm helps them convey that their words matter too.

With children or younger folks, Libras might become role models for respectful speech. They might correct rude comments with statements like, "We don't talk to each other that way. Let's find kinder words." By doing this consistently, they teach the next generation that language can build bridges rather than tear people down. Their calm presence can help children feel safe sharing their own thoughts without fear of punishment.

Libras can keep a discussion balanced by summarizing what has been said. "So far, we've heard two ideas: using a smaller budget but taking more time, or spending more upfront for faster results. Let's explore each option in detail." This summary helps everyone stay on track, especially in large group chats. It also ensures no one's input gets lost. But they must also allow for a final decision eventually.

When confusion arises, Libras might ask clarifying questions: "Could you give me an example?" or "Can you explain what you meant by that word?" This prevents misunderstandings from growing. It also shows that the Libra values accurate understanding. Though some people might see repeated questions as over-cautious, Libras believe it is better to confirm than to assume. It avoids bigger issues down the line.

Libras might also offer gentle feedback, starting with something positive: "I like your approach here. One thing I might suggest is..." This technique helps the person receiving feedback feel less attacked. The Libra's aim is to keep the conversation constructive. If the other person is open, they might find it easier to accept suggestions since the Libra did not start with negativity.

When Libras talk about their own experiences, they might include other people's perspectives too. For example, "I went to the park with Sam. Sam enjoyed the flowers, while I liked the pond. We both appreciated the quiet corner to read in." By weaving in multiple viewpoints, they showcase their interest in how different people see the same event. This can make conversations richer but sometimes longer.

If Libras need to handle a big disagreement, they might arrange a calm setting for the talk—perhaps in a quiet room or over a relaxed meal. They believe setting matters. If the environment is comfortable, they feel it is easier to stay polite. They might start the talk by saying, "I want to hear your side before I share mine." This gives the other person a sense of being respected, which can reduce defensiveness.

Emotional honesty can be a barrier for Libras. They might talk around feelings instead of naming them directly. Instead of saying, "I'm hurt," they might say, "I'm a bit bothered." Or they might say nothing at all. However, naming feelings can be important for clarity. Saying, "I feel hurt because I felt left out," is more direct and allows the other person to see what is really happening. With practice, Libras can learn that polite communication can still be authentic.

The listening side of communication is just as important for Libras. They often give people the space to speak fully, which can be comforting. But if they do not set boundaries, they might end up hearing more drama or complaints than they can handle. They can kindly say, "I understand you're upset, but can we talk about solutions?" This shifts the talk from endless venting to something more balanced.

Libras might also be skilled at nonverbal communication. A simple reassuring pat on a friend's shoulder or a sympathetic expression can show support without words. In some situations, a few gestures can speak volumes. They might also watch others' gestures to sense if they feel tense or relaxed. This careful observation helps them respond in a gentle, proper way.

Confidence in communication grows when Libras recognize that their calm and fair approach is valuable. They do not have to speak like someone else. They can keep their sense of courtesy while learning to be firm when needed. That blend allows them to manage many types of conversations successfully, from friendly chats to serious talks.

In conclusion, Libras thrive on kind, well-balanced communication. They listen actively, speak politely, and try to include all voices. They often serve as mediators who bring conflicting sides together. At the same time, they must watch out for holding back their own needs, becoming overly soft, or avoiding issues that need direct words. By learning to share their true feelings, set limits, and speak with clear purpose, Libras can harness their natural talent for communication in a way that fosters understanding and respect. This helps them build stronger bonds in all areas of life, reflecting their deep-rooted wish to connect with others on fair and caring terms.

CHAPTER 13: DAILY ROUTINES FOR LIBRA

A person's daily routine can offer insight into how they manage their time, health, relationships, and personal interests. For Libra, known for seeking balance and harmony, daily life often includes careful planning so that no single activity overwhelms the rest. This chapter will explore what a typical day might look like for a Libra, focusing on routines that match their natural wish for balance. We will look at morning habits, work or school patterns, leisure activities, and ways Libras might wind down in the evening. While every Libra is different, these ideas can point to patterns that often appear in those with Libra traits.

A Peaceful Morning

Many Libras enjoy a calm start to the day. Rather than rushing out of bed and throwing on clothes, they might prefer a gentler approach. For instance, they could set their alarm a bit earlier so they have time to stretch or do a simple breathing exercise before leaving the bedroom. This helps a Libra center their thoughts and avoid jumping into the day with stress.

Some Libras might listen to soft music or open a window to let in fresh air. They might take a moment to look outside, noticing the light and feeling thankful for a new day. Because they like harmony, Libras may arrange their bedroom so that the area near their bed feels clean and neat, allowing them to wake up in a peaceful setting.

Healthy Breakfast Choices

A balanced breakfast is often important for Libras, as they want to start the day feeling steady. They might include fruits, a source of protein like eggs or yogurt, and perhaps some whole grains. If they have more time, they might prepare a simple meal rather than grabbing something rushed. This is not to say Libras always follow perfect nutrition, but many do appreciate a meal that feels balanced in flavor and nutrition.

To keep the morning meal calm, a Libra might want to sit down rather than eat while walking around or driving. If they live with others, they could enjoy a brief chat about the day's plans, checking that everyone feels ready for what lies ahead. This small bit of connection can help a Libra feel emotionally balanced before stepping outside.

Planning the Day

After breakfast, Libras might quickly review their plan for the day. They could look at a calendar or to-do list, making sure they have not forgotten any tasks. Because Libras value fairness, they might plan enough time for each priority, whether it is school, work, family, or errands. They dislike feeling rushed, so building small breaks between tasks can keep them relaxed.

If they notice a potential clash, such as two meetings close together, a Libra might try to adjust the schedule early rather than wait until the last minute. This helps them keep their day from tipping into chaos. Some Libras also factor in time for quiet reflection or personal reading, even if it is just 15 minutes, because they see mental peace as part of the balance they need.

Commute and Transitions

Libras who commute to work or school might use that time for calm reflection. If traveling by bus or train, they might listen to gentle music, read, or watch the passing scenery. This can help them enter the next part of the day without feeling harried. If driving, they might pick a playlist that helps them stay alert yet relaxed.

If the commute is long, a Libra may use it as a chance to gather thoughts, plan upcoming tasks, or send kind messages to friends. However, they should keep an eye on stress levels—if the commute is busy, it might add tension. Finding small ways to make the commute more pleasant, such as carpooling with a friend or listening to an audiobook, can help a Libra feel that the day flows more smoothly.

Approach to Work or School

Once they arrive at work or school, Libras often show polite communication and a desire to help. Their daily routine may include greeting coworkers, classmates, or teachers in a friendly way. Libras might also find a brief moment to organize their workspace or desk, putting away anything leftover from the previous day so they start fresh.

During school hours or a work shift, Libras value fairness. They might stand up for a classmate if they see them being treated wrongly, or they might offer to help a coworker finish a project if the workload feels unbalanced. These small efforts align with a Libra's goal of keeping the environment calm and respectful.

Libras can do well with structured breaks. If the job or class schedule allows, they might step away from their desk or classroom for a short walk or a bit of stretching. This resets their focus and keeps them from feeling weighed down by continuous tasks.

Social Connections During the Day

Because Libras often enjoy good company, they might plan short social moments, such as a shared lunch or a friendly chat with peers. If they have limited time, they might still message a close friend, making sure they do not lose touch. Libras usually thrive when they feel connected, but they also try to keep social time fair—meaning they do not want to neglect tasks.

When disagreements happen at school or work, a Libra may try to settle things in a calm manner. This might include suggesting a quick meeting where each person can speak. While this can be helpful, Libras should watch that they do not spend all their energy solving others' conflicts. Setting boundaries is important for keeping a balanced routine.

Midday Pause

Around midday, many Libras appreciate a break. If possible, they might step outside for a few minutes to enjoy fresh air. Some Libras might find a quiet spot to read a few pages of a book, scroll through pleasant photos, or do a short relaxation technique. The idea is to shift away from the morning's busyness and recharge for the afternoon.

Lunch might mirror breakfast in that Libras try to choose a balanced meal. Even if they eat quickly, they often prefer a dish that is not too heavy or greasy, so they can keep energy steady. They might add a small dessert if it fits their daily plan, but they try not to overdo it. Maintaining a moderate approach feels right to many Libras.

Afternoon Productivity

During the afternoon, Libras may focus on tasks that require collaboration or communication. They could excel in group projects, negotiations, or discussions with clients. Their ability to see both sides of a situation can help them suggest fair compromises.

If working alone, a Libra might need to stay on top of time management. Their quest for the perfect solution can lead them to review details too often. To avoid that, they might set mini-deadlines, such as finishing a report by a specific hour, so they do not get lost in minor adjustments. This is where their daily routine can keep them on track, reminding them that a good result within the time limit is better than endless tweaks.

Handling Stress Points

If the day brings sudden stress—like unexpected tasks or conflicts—Libras might take a brief moment to gather themselves. They could do a quick breathing exercise, counting to five with each inhale and exhale. This can prevent them from reacting impulsively. They might also talk to a supportive friend or coworker if the situation feels overwhelming.

Some Libras keep a small notebook or app for jotting down any worries, so they can address them later without letting those thoughts crowd their mind all day. By naming the concern—"I need to fix this billing issue," for instance—they can plan a calm approach. This helps them remain steady rather than frazzled.

Early Evening Transition

As the work or school day ends, Libras might do a quick review of what they achieved and what remains for tomorrow. They could tidy their workspace or gather any items they need to take home. They might also take a moment to thank a coworker or classmate who helped them, as showing gratitude can boost everyone's mood.

The commute back home might again be a time for relaxation. If the day was stressful, a Libra might pick soothing music or a casual podcast. This helps them wind down mentally. By the time they arrive home, they hope to feel ready for personal or family time without carrying too much tension.

Home and Family Time

Evenings can be special for Libras, who value close relationships. They might spend time with family, housemates, or a partner, chatting about the day's highlights and challenges. If they live alone, they could call or message friends to maintain that social bond.

Because they like balance, Libras often try to share household tasks. They might cook dinner one night while someone else handles it another night. Or, if living alone, they might plan easy meals so they do not spend the entire evening in the kitchen. A Libra often feels satisfied when each person in the household does a fair share, preventing anyone from feeling overworked.

Personal Relaxation or Hobbies

A healthy Libra routine often includes personal interests in the evening. This might be reading, painting, playing an instrument, or working on a modest creative project. Some Libras enjoy gentle exercise, such as a short yoga session or a calm walk, to let go of any worries.

This personal time is not just for fun; it also helps a Libra recharge emotionally. If they have had a day filled with social interactions, a bit of quiet can restore their sense of balance. Conversely, if they spent the day working alone, they might choose a group activity, such as a small gathering with friends, to feel socially satisfied.

Evening Reflection

Libras may spend a few minutes looking back on the day, thinking about what went well and what could be improved. Some write in a simple journal, noting positive moments—like a kind conversation or a productive meeting—as well as small hiccups that might need attention later. This reflection can help them see patterns and adjust their routine in the future.

They might also look ahead at tomorrow's to-do list, removing anything that is no longer necessary or adding important tasks. This practice keeps them from feeling surprised when they wake up, supporting that morning sense of calm they value so much.

Social Media and Screen Time

Many Libras like to stay in touch through social media, but they also try not to let it consume their entire evening. If scrolling starts to feel like a time drain or stirs up negative emotions, a Libra might set a limit—"I'll check messages for 20 minutes, then log off." This boundary helps them maintain mental balance and avoid stress caused by too much online comparison or arguments.

Similarly, before bedtime, Libras might reduce bright screens or pick calming content to read. Their aim is to let the mind settle rather than rev up with exciting or intense information.

Nighttime Routine

As bedtime nears, Libras appreciate a relaxing routine. They might take a warm shower or bath to soothe tension from the day. A short session of stretching can loosen tight muscles, especially if they have been sitting for long hours. Some Libras enjoy using gentle scents or soft lighting in their bedroom to create a restful atmosphere.

If they share the space with a partner or family member, they might talk softly about lighter topics or read together. If alone, they could read a book or listen to calm music. Aiming for a regular bedtime helps Libras maintain their overall sense of balance. They know that lack of sleep can disrupt their mood and energy, leading to a less peaceful following day.

Weekend and Leisure Routines

Weekends or off-days can look different for Libras, but the principle of balance often remains. They might schedule a mix of social activities and personal downtime. They could visit a friend or family member for a few hours, then spend the evening relaxing at home. If they have errands, they try to space them out so the weekend does not feel hectic.

Some Libras might plan a short trip to a nearby park or a peaceful spot in nature, appreciating the chance to refresh. Others might stay at home organizing things that got messy during the week. They might also explore creative hobbies more deeply on weekends, turning their free time into a period of gentle self-expression.

Physical Wellness

Libras often see the link between physical and emotional balance. They might include moderate exercise in their routine, such as a morning or evening walk, yoga class, or a simple workout at home. They do not always aim for extreme fitness but prefer steady, doable routines that keep them feeling healthy.

Hydration is another simple way Libras might care for themselves, keeping water nearby throughout the day. Because they can forget about their own needs when focusing on others, setting small reminders to drink water or stretch can be very helpful. Feeling physically balanced often leads to a better mood and steadier energy.

Emotional Care in the Daily Routine

Throughout the day, Libras benefit from noticing their emotions. If they feel anxious or upset, they might pause and ask, "Why am I feeling this way? Is there a small step I can take to address it?" This check-in can prevent negative emotions from piling up.

Some Libras might do a short reflection at midday if they find themselves becoming irritable or tired. By naming the feeling—"I'm a bit overwhelmed"—and thinking of a quick fix—like a five-minute walk or a few calm breaths—they can return to balance. This emotional awareness is a key part of how Libras cope with daily life challenges.

Adaptability and Change

Of course, no day goes perfectly as planned. A Libra might get stuck in traffic, face a sudden deadline, or deal with a loved one's crisis. In those moments, flexibility helps. A Libra might say, "I'll rearrange my tasks and handle the priority first." They try to stay calm, knowing that occasional changes are part of life.

Over time, Libras learn that a routine is not a rigid schedule but a guide that can be adjusted. They might keep some anchors—like a morning stretch, midday check-in, and calm bedtime ritual—while adapting the hours between for new tasks or surprises. This approach keeps them from feeling trapped by unexpected events.

Examples of a Balanced Day

To provide a short outline, here is a possible daily schedule for a Libra:

7:00 AM: Wake up, do a gentle stretch, and enjoy a simple breakfast.

7:30 AM: Briefly review the day's tasks or goals.

8:00 AM: Commute or prepare for school/work, perhaps listening to calming music.

9:00 AM–12:00 PM: Focused work or classes, communicating politely with others, taking a short break as needed.

12:00 PM–1:00 PM: Lunch, possibly with friends or coworkers. A quick walk afterward.

1:00 PM–5:00 PM: Afternoon tasks, group projects, or personal study. Possibly a second break to clear the mind.

5:30 PM: Commute home, using the time for reflection or light entertainment.

6:00 PM–8:00 PM: Home tasks, cooking, or shared time with family. Some personal hobbies if there is time.

8:00 PM–9:00 PM: Relaxation—reading, music, or gentle exercise.

9:00 PM–10:00 PM: Wind down for bed, possibly journaling or chatting with a loved one.

10:00 PM: Lights out, aiming for enough sleep.

Social Balance

During a typical week, a Libra might schedule social events to ensure they see friends or extended family. They might plan a coffee catch-up or a small gathering. This fuels their need for connection while also letting them pace themselves so they are not overbooked. If a Libra notices they have social plans every night, they might block off an evening or two for solitude to keep things even.

Household and Personal Obligations

Libras also juggle chores and personal errands. They might create small time blocks to handle tasks like laundry, bill payments, or cleaning. Because they value fairness, they expect everyone in the household to do their part. If living alone, they still aim to keep chores in balance so they do not pile up. A Libra might say, "I'll do a quick tidy each day so it doesn't become a massive chore on the weekend."

Staying Motivated

Sometimes, the desire to keep everything balanced can lead a Libra to feel stuck or uncertain about what to do first. They might remedy this by setting clear goals and reminding themselves that small steps can lead to steady progress. If they see they are behind on a major task, they can break it into smaller parts: "This evening, I'll handle the first part, tomorrow the second." This keeps them motivated without feeling weighed down.

Minimizing Distractions

Because Libras can get drawn into friendly chats or online browsing, they might need to manage distractions. For instance, they could set a timer for 30 minutes of focused work followed by a 5-minute break to check messages. This strategy ensures they do not lose track of time in social media or long conversations. Maintaining a fair division between work and rest helps a Libra's day feel balanced rather than chaotic.

Routines for Self-Care

Self-care is essential for Libras. Along with physical and social habits, they might practice mental self-care. This could be reading motivational articles, learning a new skill, or watching something that uplifts their mood. They try not to let guilt stop them from taking a rest or enjoying a hobby, because they know that recharging keeps them at their best when helping others.

Habit Tracking

Some Libras find it helpful to track habits, like drinking enough water, spending quality time with loved ones, or sticking to a bedtime. They might use an app or a notebook to mark off each day's progress. This can be motivating because it shows patterns—maybe they sleep better when they turn off screens early, or they feel calmer when they fit in a short walk. Adjusting habits in small ways can lead to a smoother, more harmonious routine overall.

Evening Gratitude

Right before sleep, a Libra might reflect on what they are thankful for, such as supportive friends, a positive achievement at work, or simply a peaceful moment in the day. This gentle exercise can shift their mind away from stress or worries, helping them drift off with a feeling of calm. If they share a home with someone, they might exchange a kind word about something they each appreciated that day.

Adjusting for Life Stages

Daily routines can look different for Libras in various life stages—children, teenagers, college students, young professionals, parents, or retirees. Yet the theme of seeking balance tends to remain. A college-age Libra might juggle classes, part-time work, and social activities, while a retired Libra might fill the day with volunteer work, hobbies, or family visits. In each stage, they adapt the routine to meet new goals but still aim to keep the overall sense of order.

Handling Surprises and Setbacks

No matter how well-planned a routine is, surprises happen. A Libra might face an illness, a family emergency, or a sudden work request. In those cases, the routine might need a quick rewrite. Libras who practice flexibility can handle these twists with less distress. They might keep a calm voice, tell themselves, "Let's address the priority first," and then return to their routine as soon as it is reasonable. Accepting that life sometimes disrupts balance is part of staying emotionally steady.

Vacation or Break Times

Vacations can be wonderful for Libras as they get a chance to relax or explore new places. They might aim for an itinerary that includes both peaceful downtime and light sightseeing. If traveling with friends, the Libra might mediate the schedule so that each person's interests are included. They do not want anyone to feel left out or bored.

Listening to the Body

Throughout the day, Libras might pay attention to physical signals. If they feel hungry early, they might have a small snack to avoid a mood dip. If they realize they are tense, they might do a brief stretch. This helps prevent minor discomfort from turning into bigger problems. Over time, Libras can grow more mindful of how their body reacts to stress, rest, and meals, adjusting accordingly.

Balancing Others' Needs with Their Own

A Libra's routine often involves interacting with people. They might help a friend with a project, support a family member, or join a community group. However, they must remember not to neglect their own tasks. If they spend all evening helping someone else, they might feel drained or behind on personal chores. Keeping a fair split of time between self and others is key for staying emotionally healthy.

Reflection on Improvement

At the end of the week, some Libras do a broader reflection. They might notice if they felt rushed too often or if they had enough social contact. Then they can fine-tune the upcoming week: "I'll go to bed earlier on Wednesday," or "I'll add a half-hour phone call with my grandma on Friday." These small changes help them craft a routine that matches their needs and values.

Steady Growth Over Time

As Libras gain life experience, they typically refine their daily patterns. They might learn that too many back-to-back appointments create stress, or that skipping breakfast makes them cranky. Through trial and error, they shape a routine that keeps them at peace. While they might switch jobs, move homes, or shift social circles, the central idea—finding balance—stays consistent.

Tips for Keeping a Libra Routine

Start with a calm morning: Even five minutes of quiet sets a gentle tone.

Keep tasks organized: A schedule or list prevents forgetting duties and helps avoid rushing.

Create short breaks: Rest or stretch every few hours to maintain energy.

Stay flexible: Accept that plans change and adapt without too much worry.

Share tasks fairly: At home or work, aim for an even distribution.

Reflect daily: A few minutes of review can guide improvements.

Value your own needs: Balance time for others with personal care.

Avoiding Common Pitfalls

Sometimes, Libras might try to fit too much into a single day because they want to meet all requests. This can lead to burnout. Learning to say "I can't do this today, but maybe another time" protects them. Another pitfall is perfectionism—spending forever on a small detail and missing other important tasks. Setting limits keeps them moving forward without losing their sense of harmony.

Conclusion on Daily Routines

A Libra's day often reflects their core desire for evenness, calm, and fairness. From a gentle wake-up to a peaceful bedtime, they try to include enough rest, social contact, work or school efforts, and personal interests. Though real life can be messy, Libras cope by planning small anchors—like a mindful breakfast or a brief evening reflection—that keep them steady in a busy world. With experience, they learn to adapt these routines so they remain effective and uplifting, ensuring that each day has a sense of calm flow rather than frantic imbalance.

In the end, a Libra's routine is about more than just tasks. It is a reflection of their guiding principles: kindness, fairness, and the wish to remain stable amid change. By noticing their energy levels, planning time wisely, and sharing responsibilities with others, Libras can shape a daily life that feels rewarding and harmonious. This approach helps them stay true to their sign's focus on balance while still handling the real demands of everyday life.

CHAPTER 14: MISUNDERSTANDINGS ABOUT LIBRA

Even though many people see Libra as friendly, fair, and calm, there are some misconceptions about this sign. These misunderstandings can arise from generalizations, stereotypes, or oversimplified horoscopes. In this chapter, we will look at common mistakes people make about Libras, explaining why those views are not always correct. We will also explore the true variety in Libra personalities and how these individuals might respond to each misconception.

Misconception 1: Libras Never Feel Strong Emotions

One of the most repeated misunderstandings is that Libras are always calm and do not experience intense feelings. People might think that Libras, being the "balanced" sign, never get very angry, sad, or excited. In reality, Libras do feel a range of emotions. They simply choose to manage those emotions in a polite or controlled way. They may avoid yelling or crying in public, but that does not mean the feelings are absent.

Often, Libras deal with strong emotions privately. They might talk to a close friend, write in a journal, or find comfort in music. This quiet method of handling feelings can cause others to assume Libras are emotionless or lukewarm. It is more accurate to say that Libras care about harmony, so they try not to let emotions escalate into chaos unless they cannot avoid it.

Misconception 2: Libras Are Always Indecisive

Another frequent claim is that Libras can never make up their minds. While Libras do weigh options carefully, calling them perpetually indecisive oversimplifies. Many Libras can and do make firm choices, especially when they have enough information or when their personal values point clearly to one path.

The confusion likely arises from the fact that Libras want a fair outcome, so they look at multiple angles before deciding. Yes, this can take time. But once Libras recognize the best route (or the fairest solution), they can act with confidence. In addition, practice and life experience help Libras become quicker at deciding without endless back-and-forth.

Misconception 3: Libras Only Care About Appearances

Some think Libras, being linked to beauty through the planet Venus, are shallow or overly focused on looks. While it is true that many Libras have an eye for harmony in fashion, art, or design, that does not mean they are superficial. They might enjoy pleasant surroundings but still hold deep values and interests.

For instance, a Libra could love decorating their room in a coordinated style while also reading about social issues or studying advanced subjects. Their appreciation of beauty is part of wanting balance, not a sign of vanity. They might feel that a tidy and visually pleasing space helps them stay calm and centered. This is different from caring about appearances just to impress others.

Misconception 4: Libras Are Fake or Insincere

Because Libras often speak politely and aim to keep the peace, some people accuse them of being insincere—thinking they say "nice" things without truly meaning them. While it is true that Libras usually avoid blunt or hurtful remarks, they can still be genuine.

They simply prefer to phrase things gently, especially if something might lead to conflict.

The difference between polite kindness and fake flattery is subtle. A sincere Libra might offer compliments that reflect real appreciation. However, if they believe a direct criticism would do more harm than good, they might rephrase it in a gentle way. That is not necessarily being fake; it is a chosen communication style meant to preserve goodwill. Of course, some individuals (of any sign) can be phony, but it is unfair to claim all Libras are that way.

Misconception 5: Libras Must Be Social Butterflies

Many horoscopes describe Libras as very outgoing, always seeking parties or group gatherings. In truth, while many Libras do like being around people, not all are extroverted. Some prefer small, one-on-one settings or enjoy only a limited circle of friends. The common factor is the desire for harmonious connections, not necessarily a constant crowd.

An introverted Libra might have a few close companions and still show the typical Libra traits of fairness and calm. They might choose cozy meetups rather than large parties. So the idea that every Libra is a chatty extrovert is a myth. Personality factors like upbringing, personal history, and interests can shape how social a Libra becomes.

Misconception 6: Libras Avoid Conflict Because They Are Weak

It is often said that Libras dislike conflict and will do anything to evade it. Some interpret this as weakness or cowardice. In reality, Libras can be quite strong-willed but simply choose diplomacy first. They do not see yelling or direct confrontation as the best path unless it becomes necessary.

When a vital issue of fairness arises, Libras can stand up firmly. They may speak calmly but refuse to back down if they believe something is unjust. Their preference for peace does not equal an inability to defend themselves or others. In many cases, it takes considerable strength to keep calm in tough conversations, rather than lashing out.

Misconception 7: Libras Are People-Pleasers All the Time

Because Libras aim for balanced relationships, some assume they only say what others want to hear, never expressing personal wants. But while Libras do care about not hurting feelings, they often still have strong ideas of their own. They might phrase those ideas gently, making sure the other side feels respected.

People might see that courtesy and assume the Libra is just agreeing. In truth, the Libra could be finding points of agreement before presenting their own stance. Over time, Libras learn to be clearer about personal needs so they do not get overlooked. They aim for a solution that respects everyone, including themselves.

Misconception 8: All Libras Are the Same

This is a broad myth for any zodiac sign. People might say, "You're a Libra, so you must act exactly this way." But humans are shaped by far more than just their sun sign—upbringing, culture, personal experiences, and other astrological factors (like moon sign or rising sign) can differ. Two Libras might share some traits yet express them in very different ways.

For example, one Libra might be quite talkative, applying fairness in group settings. Another might be quieter, showing fairness through attentive listening and well-chosen words. Both can still be considered Libras with a focus on harmony, but their day-to-day behaviors might not match perfectly.

Misconception 9: Libras Can Only Work in Social or Artistic Fields

Some people assume that since Libra is ruled by Venus, every Libra must be an artist, designer, or social coordinator. While many do excel in creative or interpersonal roles, Libras can succeed in a variety of careers. There are Libras who become scientists, engineers, or accountants, using their sense of balance to handle logic-based jobs.

What remains consistent is that Libras often seek fairness and calm in any workplace. Whether they design buildings or handle finances, they might approach the job with a methodical, balanced viewpoint. They could aim to build good relationships with coworkers, but that does not limit their career to "artistic" alone.

Why These Misconceptions Appear

One reason these misconceptions arise is the simplified descriptions in newspapers or quick online horoscopes, which often paint signs in bold strokes. Another reason is that Libras themselves sometimes project a calm exterior that hides deeper feelings or complexities. Observers might jump to conclusions if they only see the polite outer layer.

Also, some folks like to tease Libras about indecision or a love of pretty things. Over time, jokes can become stereotypes. It is wise to remember that each person is unique, and astrological signs only offer one angle of understanding human behavior.

How Libras Can Respond to Misconceptions

A Libra who hears these myths can handle them in a diplomatic way. If someone says, "Oh, you must be indecisive," the Libra might smile and explain, "I do like to consider options thoroughly, but I can decide once I know what matters most." This brief explanation can clear up false ideas without hostility.

If teased for always being nice, a Libra might calmly point out a situation where they stood firm. "I spoke up in that meeting when something was unfair," they could say. This helps people see that the Libra's kindness does not mean they are a pushover. By offering examples of deeper traits, Libras can gently counter misunderstandings.

The Risk of Self-Fulfilling Prophecies

If a Libra grows up hearing they must be polite or that they must never show anger because "that's how Libras are," they could become overly cautious or hide feelings. This can lead them to deny valid emotions or avoid confrontation even when needed. Over time, these behaviors can cause frustration and confusion.

Recognizing that astrological signs are not absolute destiny can help a Libra break free from limiting labels. They can learn healthy ways to express anger, sadness, or strong opinions without feeling they are betraying their sign. True balance means addressing problems openly, not avoiding them out of fear.

Individual Differences in Libras

There are bold Libras who speak their mind clearly. There are quiet Libras who prefer subtlety. Some Libras adore fashion and design; others care little for aesthetics and focus on mental pursuits. Each of these expressions can still carry the root Libra qualities: a desire for harmony, fairness, and calm. The sign does not lock a person into a single mold.

Furthermore, outside factors such as early family environment can shape how a Libra appears. If a Libra grew up in a loud, argumentative home, they might react by becoming very quiet or, conversely, by learning to argue politely. Both are valid adaptations that do not remove their Libra traits.

Myth of Eternal Balance

A big misconception is that Libras are always perfectly balanced. In truth, Libras struggle with imbalance just like everyone else. They might feel stressed, overcommit, or become moody when life gets hectic. The difference is that Libras are often aware of the imbalance and try to fix it. They might reorganize their schedule, talk things out with a friend, or adjust their environment to regain calm.

Calling Libras "perfectly balanced all the time" sets unrealistic expectations. It can be stressful for a Libra to feel they must never let others see them upset or disorganized. In reality, Libras have highs and lows, but they aim to correct the lows rather than remain in them.

Misconception 10: Libras Are Obsessed with Romance

While many Libras do value partnerships, it is inaccurate to claim they are obsessed with love or cannot function alone. Libras often like companionship because they appreciate shared harmony, but that does not mean they jump into any relationship just to avoid being by themselves.

A Libra may actually be picky, wanting a partner who respects fairness and communication. They might stay single for a while if they do not find someone who matches their values. So the myth that a Libra is desperate for romance at all costs misses the truth that Libras often seek quality over quick pairings.

Stereotypes in Compatibility

People sometimes say Libras can only get along with certain signs, such as Gemini or Aquarius, and can never pair well with others. This black-and-white view can be misleading. While some sign pairings might have common ground, real compatibility depends on individual personalities, shared interests, and willingness to compromise.

A Libra could form a healthy bond with a sign that is traditionally considered challenging, like Capricorn or Scorpio, if both parties respect each other's differences. The idea that "all Libras must date these signs and avoid those signs" overlooks the complexity of real relationships.

Misconception 11: Libras Lack Depth

Because Libras often handle emotions or conflicts gently, some people think they do not have depth. This is not true. Many Libras engage deeply with music, art, philosophical questions, or personal reflection. They can be thoughtful thinkers, analyzing how to achieve justice in social issues or how to be a better friend.

The outward politeness might mask a passionate spirit about certain causes, like fairness at work, treatment of animals, or equal opportunities. Libras may pour significant energy into these passions. They simply maintain a calm approach while pursuing them.

Handling Criticism and Labels

If a Libra faces repeated misconceptions, they can respond by calmly sharing examples of how they actually behave. For instance, if told "You never show anger," they might explain a time they stood up in a heated situation. Being polite does not mean a Libra allows injustice.

Another option is to let actions speak louder than words. If someone expects the Libra to be indecisive, the Libra can make a clear choice in a discussion, demonstrating that they do not always hesitate. Over time, consistent behavior can break down stereotypes.

Embracing Complexity

Ultimately, Libras are complex individuals. They are not just "the balanced one" or "the indecisive one." They have a range of traits: empathy, a longing for fairness, communication skills, and sometimes struggles with setting boundaries or showing anger. Recognizing this complexity allows Libras to be more confident in who they are, without feeling trapped by others' assumptions.

Misconception 12: Libras Rely on Others to Make Them Happy

Because Libras value social harmony, some assume they cannot be content alone. Actually, while Libras thrive on healthy connections, many also enjoy personal time. They might read, do crafts, or relax in a quiet space. They see relationships as a source of joy, but not the only path to well-being.

Yes, Libras may feel uneasy if conflicts strain their bonds, but that is because conflict disrupts their sense of peace. They can still find internal comfort in solitary activities. A balanced Libra recognizes that self-sufficiency and companionship can coexist.

The Danger of Oversimplified Horoscopes

Quick horoscope tidbits might say, "Libras are charming but can't decide anything." If a reader only sees these short lines, they might believe every Libra is flighty. Real astrology texts often note the positives and negatives, stating that Libras can be quite decisive once they analyze a situation, and that their charm comes from a genuine wish to be kind. Looking deeper than short blurbs can reveal the full picture.

Showing the Real Libra

Libras themselves can break misconceptions by openly discussing their motivations. For instance, if they speak kindly in a tense moment, they might later say, "I wanted to find a fair solution, not brush aside the problem." This helps others understand that their calm approach is a deliberate choice, not a sign of fear or naivety.

They can also share their passions or deeper thoughts. Friends might be surprised to learn a Libra is deeply knowledgeable about science, history, or social justice. By expressing these interests, Libras show they are not just about polite conversation or pleasing aesthetics.

Misconception 13: Libras Run from Responsibility

Some might think that because Libras dislike conflict, they also avoid tough responsibilities. However, Libras are often reliable team players. They can handle tasks with diligence, ensuring that details are correct and people are treated fairly. They just prefer to solve problems cooperatively.

If a leadership role requires direct commands, a Libra might find it challenging at first, but many adapt by balancing a friendly tone with firm direction. This does not mean they run from responsibility; they simply approach it with a style that preserves harmony.

Misconception 14: Libras Are Too Soft to Manage Stress

Another myth is that Libras fold under pressure because they want everything calm. In fact, many Libras excel in high-pressure situations by staying composed. Their ability to keep a level head can help them in crises—such as mediating disputes or leading a project during a crunch time.

They might feel stress internally, but they manage it with deep breaths, structured thinking, or quiet breaks. Their outward calm can reassure others. This skill is far from being "soft." It is a refined approach that values efficiency without letting emotions explode.

How Misconceptions Affect Libras

Repeatedly being labeled can frustrate Libras, especially if they are misunderstood in social groups, at work, or by relatives. They might feel pigeonholed as "the nice one" or "the person who can't decide." Over time, they could either try too hard to disprove the labels or withdraw to avoid conflict.

A healthier path is to accept that such labels exist but do not define them fully. Libras can keep communicating their true selves and set boundaries when teased or misjudged. If friends or family persist in using harmful stereotypes, the Libra might calmly remind them, "You know I'm more than that."

Encouraging Others to See Beyond Stereotypes

People close to a Libra can help dispel myths by noticing the Libra's real actions. For instance, if a Libra friend organizes a gathering smoothly, that counters the notion that Libras are paralyzed by indecision. If a Libra coworker calmly handles a tough client, that shows they are not unable to cope with stress.

The more real examples people observe, the more they realize that superficial stereotypes do not capture the Libra's complexity. Over time, these positive encounters shape a broader understanding of what Libras can do.

Learning from Misconceptions

Libras themselves might reflect on which myths bother them the most. Is it the idea they are shallow, or that they cannot decide anything? By knowing which falsehood stings the most, they can practice clarifying that part of their identity. They can also see if any grain of truth exists—maybe they do hesitate too long sometimes, or focus on appearances—then work on growth in those areas.

As with any sign, no one is perfect. Recognizing a small real issue inside a bigger myth might lead a Libra to self-improvement. For example, if they do struggle with overthinking decisions, they might learn strategies to become more decisive. This is different from fully accepting the label "indecisive" as destiny.

Embracing Real Strengths and Weaknesses

Libras can embrace that fairness, empathy, and calm are genuine strengths. They can also admit that they sometimes avoid direct conflict or take extra time to pick a course of action. Recognizing these traits honestly allows them to respond to misconceptions without shame or denial.

People who respect the Libra's balanced viewpoint might see how it fosters healthy relationships and good teamwork. Those who misunderstand might label it as weakness. By calmly explaining their reasoning, Libras show that what appears as "weak" is often careful thought.

Avoiding Negative Self-Talk

Sometimes, Libras might internalize myths and start doubting themselves. If they hear "You're always sitting on the fence," they might feel guilty whenever they consider multiple options. They might push themselves to make rash decisions just to avoid the label of indecision. This can lead to errors in judgment.

It helps to remember that careful thinking is not bad. It becomes a problem only if they truly cannot move forward. A Libra who sees their method as a tool can remain patient with themselves, explaining to others, "I'm looking at each detail to ensure fairness."

Saying No to Over-Generalizations

Not every Libra has the same approach to style, social life, or emotional expression. Some dress boldly; others prefer simple clothing. Some love big crowds; others want quiet dinners. Some share every feeling with a friend; others keep emotions private until trust is built.

Over-generalizations miss these differences. When someone insists, "All Libras do X," the Libra can respond with an example of how they or someone else with the same sign does not fit that mold. This can spark a more honest conversation about the variety within a single zodiac sign.

Respecting the Unique Libra Path

Each Libra's path in life—family choices, career ambitions, or personal goals—can differ greatly. Some might value creative work, while others focus on business or science. The sign's emphasis on balance and harmony can influence how they approach tasks, but not necessarily what tasks they choose.

By respecting each Libra's individuality, we avoid reducing them to a few stereotypes. Libras themselves can feel free to explore different interests without feeling locked into a so-called Libra mold. This freedom to explore fosters personal growth and a richer expression of who they truly are.

Overcoming Judgments in Relationships

In relationships, both romantic and otherwise, a partner or friend might bring along misconceptions. If the friend says, "You're such a Libra. You can't handle arguments," the Libra might calmly show how they handle disagreements with thoughtful dialogue. By modeling constructive conflict resolution, they prove that their approach is not avoidance but reasoned discussion.

Over time, the friend realizes that Libra's style can solve issues without loud fights. This can build mutual respect. The partner or friend learns not to assume the Libra will always avoid confrontation, but to appreciate the gentle yet firm stance when it truly matters.

Healthy Pride in Libra Traits

Despite the misconceptions, many Libras find pride in their ability to see multiple viewpoints, communicate politely, and foster peaceful settings. They might say, "Yes, I do aim for fairness, and I'm glad I can listen well." By embracing these qualities, they can show that being balanced is not dull or weak. It is a thoughtful approach that promotes well-being for everyone.

This pride can encourage Libras to keep refining their strengths. They might study communication techniques, learn conflict resolution, or deepen their knowledge of ethical decision-making. These pursuits align well with their core values.

Encouraging Others to Stay Open-Minded

Libras can gently nudge those around them to avoid labeling others by zodiac sign alone. For example, if a friend says, "She's a Libra, so she's probably vain," the Libra can respond, "I'm a Libra too, but I'm not that way. Everyone is different." This small reminder broadens the friend's perspective.

Similarly, Libras can highlight times when people break stereotypes, not just about Libra but about all signs. This fosters a more nuanced view of astrology as a guide rather than a strict rulebook.

Reflecting on Positive Libra Traits

While debunking myths, it is worth remembering the genuine strengths Libras bring to the table: diplomacy, fairness, collaboration, an eye for harmony, and a willingness to consider all angles. These can be powerful tools in building respectful communities, workplaces, and families.

If critics say, "You're too nice," Libras might point out how that kindness often defuses tension or helps shy people speak up. By reframing "nice" as "supportive and respectful," they give credit to the very trait others might underestimate.

Adapting Misconceptions for Personal Growth

Sometimes, hearing a misconception can be a chance for self-reflection. If a Libra is called indecisive, they might pause to see if they are indeed stuck in a cycle of overthinking. If so, they can practice quicker decision-making strategies. If not, they can let the comment go, recognizing it as a false assumption.

Similarly, if someone says Libras avoid conflict, a Libra can reflect: "Am I ignoring problems? Or am I handling them calmly?" If they realize they truly are avoiding, they can work on facing difficult topics more directly. This turns a negative label into an opportunity for growth.

The Ongoing Process of Understanding

Misunderstandings do not vanish overnight. Libras might find the same myths repeated by different people over time. Rather than feeling discouraged, they can see each instance as a chance to clarify. Gradually, those close to the Libra will learn the truth of their nature.

Over time, friends and family might even defend the Libra's reputation, saying things like, "They're not indecisive—they just like to make sure everyone's ideas are heard first." This is when the Libra knows their actions have changed minds for the better.

CHAPTER 15: LIBRA AND PERSONAL INTERESTS

Each Libra has unique interests, but there are some common themes in the hobbies and activities they might explore. Because Libra often focuses on harmony and beauty, they could lean toward pursuits that let them create pleasing sights, sounds, or feelings. Still, plenty of Libras may also enjoy physical activities, problem-solving, or other areas. In this chapter, we will look at how Libras might pick personal interests, how they approach their hobbies, and how they keep things balanced while enjoying what they love.

Creative Hobbies and Art

Many Libras have a fondness for art or design. This does not mean every Libra is an artist, but they might admire beauty in paintings, decorations, or crafts. Some Libras find happiness in drawing, painting, or making handmade items. They might not always aim to become professionals; they could simply enjoy creating something pleasant to look at. This aligns with Libra's link to Venus, which people often say brings a sense of charm and a desire for loveliness.

Music and Libra

Music can be another strong interest. A Libra might learn to play an instrument, sing in a choir, or just listen to tunes that match their mood. Some find that music helps them stay calm when life gets busy. Others enjoy playing in a band or a small group because it blends creativity with teamwork. The Libra's sense of cooperation can shine in such settings, as they try to make sure each member's part fits nicely together.

Reading and Writing

Libras often like to share ideas, and reading is one way to gather fresh thoughts. They might read fiction with vivid descriptions, since that can give them a sense of pleasing imagery. Alternatively, they might explore books on social topics, fairness, or personal growth. Writing could also appeal to them, especially if it involves describing characters and settings in a balanced, thoughtful style. Some Libras keep personal journals where they record observations or reflect on daily events in a calm, clear voice.

Fashion and Style

Many Libras enjoy expressing themselves through clothing or accessories. They might not always wear fancy outfits, but they do appreciate harmony in colors or patterns. A Libra might like matching certain items or picking outfits that look coordinated. This does not have to be pricey; even a simple style with neat lines can suit them. Because Libras aim for balance, they try not to overdo patterns or colors. They want to maintain a look that feels just right—neither too plain nor too loud.

Culinary Pursuits

Cooking or baking can be a fun way for Libras to bring beauty and balance into something practical. A Libra might enjoy arranging food on a plate so that it looks appealing. They could try recipes that blend flavors in a balanced way—maybe sweet with a slight tang, or savory with a note of freshness. If they cook for friends, they will try to ensure everyone gets to eat something they like, reflecting the Libra's desire for fairness.

Gardening and Nature

Some Libras feel at ease when they spend time outdoors. They might enjoy planting flowers or herbs, tending to them patiently, and watching them grow. The result can be a small garden with pleasing shapes and colors. Tending plants can also give Libras a quiet break from busy routines, letting them breathe fresh air and stay grounded. Even a few potted plants on a balcony can satisfy their sense of calm.

Strategic Games

Because Libra is an air sign, it is sometimes associated with thinking and cleverness. Libras might like puzzles, board games, or strategy games where they weigh options. They enjoy analyzing both sides of a move, trying to guess what might happen. Such games let them exercise their careful decision-making in a relaxed setting. They can also build friendships through these activities, since Libras like playing together in a fair and friendly way.

Physical Activities

Not all Libras focus on calm hobbies. Some enjoy physical movement, especially activities that involve graceful motion or teamwork. For example, they might try dancing—ballet, modern dance, or a social style like salsa—because it blends music, movement, and cooperation. Others might prefer a gentle sport such as tennis or badminton, which requires strategy and keeps the body active without being too rough. The point is to find a balanced exercise that feels pleasing rather than extremely aggressive.

Volunteering and Community Projects

Some Libras express their personal interests by helping out in their community. They could join a local group that organizes fairs or small gatherings. They might also help in animal shelters, libraries, or after-school programs. Because fairness matters to Libras, they may feel drawn to projects that ensure equal chances for everyone. Volunteering can become a meaningful part of their life, giving them a sense that they are contributing something positive.

Cultural Exploration

Libras might be curious about different cultures, enjoying activities that teach them about music, art, or traditions from faraway places. They could visit museums, watch documentaries, or attend performances that highlight global variety. This helps them broaden their sense of balance, seeing how different societies express beauty and solve problems. By comparing these perspectives, Libras feed their natural interest in fairness and mutual respect.

Collecting

Whether it is stamps, figurines, coins, or records, collecting can appeal to a Libra's wish for orderly beauty. They might like arranging items in a way that looks nice on shelves or in albums. This hobby can show a Libra's patient side, as they carefully search for pieces to complete a set. At the same time, they must watch out for clutter if the collection grows too big—staying tidy helps maintain the calming vibe Libras prefer.

Writing Letters or Cards

In a world of quick messages, some Libras still enjoy the art of writing letters or sending cards. They might choose special paper or decorate the envelope with small designs. This method of communication can feel more personal and thoughtful, fitting the Libra's desire for warm, balanced connections. They might send letters for birthdays or other special moments, or just to say they are thinking of a friend.

Social Hobbies

Libras who are more outgoing may look for group hobbies that let them chat and share. They might join a book club, a craft circle, or a local sports team. These groups allow Libras to connect with diverse people, hear various ideas, and keep the atmosphere friendly. If a disagreement pops up, the Libra can calmly guide everyone back to harmony. This approach can be quite valuable in group settings.

Home Decorating

Arranging furniture or picking color themes for a room can be another personal interest. Some Libras love turning a space into a comfortable retreat, selecting pillows, rugs, or wall art that match in color or style. Even if they live in a small apartment, they might find joy in placing a cozy lamp in a corner or adding a splash of color with a decorative blanket. They aim for a space that feels both functional and pleasing.

Meditation and Quiet Activities

Libras sometimes choose interests that help them calm their mind. This might be simple meditation, gentle yoga, or even adult coloring books. These pursuits allow them to center their thoughts and manage any stress from daily life. An interest in quiet activities can balance out the more social parts of a Libra's day, giving them time to reflect and recharge.

Photography

Capturing images can be a fun way for a Libra to exercise their eye for symmetry. They might take pictures of landscapes, architecture, or people in natural poses. While some Libras may go all in with fancy cameras, others could simply use a phone to snap pictures of scenes that catch their eye. The process of framing a picture in a balanced way can be quite satisfying, and many Libras enjoy sharing these photos with friends.

Hosting Small Gatherings

Libras may love hosting a few friends for a calm evening at home. They might arrange simple snacks, light music, and comfortable seating. The aim is to create a setting where people can chat, laugh, and enjoy one another's company. A Libra host often makes sure everyone feels included, from food preferences to conversation topics. This gentle approach helps keep the atmosphere pleasant.

Learning New Skills

Because Libras can be curious about a range of interests, they may pick up new skills often. They might try knitting, calligraphy, or playing a new instrument. They do not always stick with every skill, but the exploration is part of the fun. Learning step by step suits Libra's careful nature, as they enjoy pacing themselves and asking for help when needed. Over time, they might gather a diverse set of abilities, reflecting their broad curiosity.

Balancing Multiple Interests

One challenge Libras face is juggling many hobbies or personal projects at once. They might start painting a canvas but also want to practice piano and read a new novel. This can become overwhelming if they do not set priorities. To keep things balanced, a Libra might schedule certain days for certain pursuits, ensuring they do not spread themselves too thin. This method helps them savor each hobby without feeling rushed.

Sharing Interests with Others

Libras often like to share their hobbies, whether it is cooking a meal for friends or playing music at a small get-together. They might show a piece of artwork they made or teach a simple craft. This sharing can spark friendly chats and let the Libra see other people's reactions. If someone else is interested, the Libra might invite them to join in or give them tips. By bringing people together around a shared interest, Libras foster the sense of harmony they love.

Self-Expression in Small Ways

Personal interests do not have to be large-scale. Even small acts—like rearranging items on a shelf so they look balanced, picking out a new phone case that fits the Libra's color scheme, or writing a short poem—can satisfy the desire for pleasing order. These tiny everyday choices reflect Libra's longing for calm patterns in life. They turn ordinary moments into a chance for gentle self-expression.

Traveling for Inspiration

If a Libra has the opportunity, exploring new places can inspire them. They might appreciate visiting museums, gardens, or historical sites, taking pictures or notes on details that catch their eye. They could also bring a sketchbook to capture interesting shapes or color combinations they see. When they return home, they might integrate these observations into their art, cooking, or design ideas.

Connecting with Like-Minded People

Many Libras enjoy discussing their interests with people who understand or share those passions. They might join online forums or groups about art, music, or crafts, or attend local events where they can meet enthusiasts. This can lead to strong friendships, as the Libra and others exchange ideas. True to Libra form, they try to ensure everyone's voice is heard in such discussions, keeping a polite tone even if opinions differ.

Challenges in Personal Interests

One issue a Libra might face is second-guessing their choices. For instance, if they begin learning guitar, they could worry they picked the "wrong" instrument. Or if they start painting with watercolors, they might wonder if they should switch to acrylics. This can slow their progress. The best approach for a Libra is to trust the joy they feel in the moment. Sticking with a hobby until they have given it a fair chance often leads to deeper satisfaction.

Perfectionism

Libras sometimes strive to create things that are perfectly balanced. If they paint, they might fuss over tiny details to get the colors just right. If they arrange a meal, they could spend a lot of time on presentation. While aiming for high standards can produce lovely results, it can also cause stress if the Libra sets the bar too high. Learning when something is "good enough" can help them actually complete projects rather than abandon them due to frustration.

Overcommitting

Another challenge occurs if a Libra says "yes" to too many group activities or clubs. Their desire to be fair and not disappoint anyone can lead them to join multiple events at once. Eventually, they might realize they do not have time for all these activities. Managing their schedule is key. By picking a few meaningful hobbies rather than many casual ones, they can stay balanced and truly enjoy each interest.

Finding Time to Recharge

Hobbies should be relaxing or invigorating, but sometimes a Libra might get so involved that they forget to rest. If they find themselves exhausted or tense, it could be a sign they need quieter moments. Even a hobby that is loved can become stressful if done in a rushed manner. Recognizing personal energy levels helps Libras keep their interests fun rather than draining.

Age and Evolving Interests

A Libra child might enjoy drawing pictures with bright colors, while a teenage Libra could explore music or drama clubs. An adult Libra might focus on home decorating or cooking, and a retired Libra might delve into gardening or volunteering. Personal interests evolve over time, but the Libra's core preference for balanced, pleasing activities often remains. They adapt as they grow, discovering new pursuits that align with life's changing demands.

Encouraging Growth

Some Libra interests also open doors to personal growth. For instance, if they love cooking, they might expand their cooking style to learn international dishes, thus broadening their cultural understanding. If they enjoy photography, they could sharpen their awareness of color and composition, which might help them in other areas like home décor. Libra's flexible mind can link one hobby to another, building a wide-ranging skillset.

Team or Solo Activities

Libras may like group hobbies, but some also prefer solitary pursuits to unwind. The choice depends on the Libra's mood and personality. A Libra who is around people all day might pick a quiet hobby at night. Another Libra, who works alone, might join a dance class or a choir for social contact. Balancing group time and alone time is crucial to staying refreshed and engaged.

Setting Realistic Goals

When starting a new personal interest, Libras benefit from setting small, realistic goals. For example, if they want to learn the guitar, they might aim to practice chords for 15 minutes daily instead of trying to master everything in a week. This steady approach fits Libra's style, reducing the pressure to be perfect. Achieving small goals also boosts confidence, encouraging them to continue.

Experimenting Without Fear

Libras sometimes hesitate to try unfamiliar activities, worried they might not excel right away. But experimentation is part of the fun. They might join a pottery class or attempt digital art. Even if the outcome looks messy at first, the process can be enjoyable and reveal hidden talents. This open-mindedness reflects Libra's love of discovery. If they do not like a hobby, that is okay. They can move on, knowing they gave it a fair shot.

Combining Interests

Sometimes, Libras merge two or more personal interests for a richer experience. For instance, a Libra who loves cooking and photography might take pictures of their dishes and share them online. Or a Libra who enjoys writing and music might write short stories set to gentle melodies. When Libras blend activities, they can express creativity in unique ways, and it can prevent boredom from doing just one thing all the time.

Encouragement from Friends and Family

Libras thrive on positive feedback, so if friends or family appreciate their art, meals, or music, it motivates them. However, Libras also try to keep their own sense of enjoyment. While praise is nice, they should not rely on it entirely. A healthy balance means doing what they love regardless of external applause. That said, sharing and receiving kind words can make the experience more fulfilling.

Connecting Hobbies to Libra Traits

Overall, the personal interests of Libras often reflect their innate love of harmony. Whether it is painting landscapes, crafting a balanced meal, or playing a group sport with friendly interaction, Libras look for activities that give a calm and positive vibe. They might also appreciate pastimes that involve fairness—like volunteer work or teaching friends a skill—because it aligns with their sense of justice.

Handling Criticism

In creative hobbies, Libras might worry about negative feedback. Because they want to keep peace, they might avoid showing their work if they fear harsh comments. But gentle, constructive criticism can help them grow. If someone suggests a tweak to their painting technique or cooking style, a Libra can view it as a chance to improve. They can stay calm by remembering that not everyone has the same taste. Over time, Libras can build resilience, using feedback to refine their craft without feeling personally attacked.

Enjoying the Process

Libras benefit from focusing on the process, not just the end result. If a Libra is learning to knit, for example, the slow, rhythmic motion can be soothing. If they are practicing a dance routine, feeling the music flow through their body can be uplifting. Rather than rushing to finish, they can let each step bring a sense of balance and calm. This mindset also helps them avoid feeling disappointed if the final outcome is not exactly what they pictured.

CHAPTER 16: LIBRA AND WELL-BEING

For a Libra, feeling good often means more than just being free of illness. It includes emotional calm, mental clarity, satisfying relationships, and a balanced daily routine. Because Libras value harmony, they tend to notice quickly if life feels off-kilter. This chapter explores how Libras might look after their well-being. We will discuss emotional balance, physical health, managing stress, and building supportive connections, all from a Libra-friendly angle.

Emotional Balance

Libras are sometimes called the "balancers" of the zodiac. They generally want their emotions to be in a steady place rather than up and down. But real life has highs and lows. When a Libra experiences sadness, anxiety, or anger, they might try to handle it quietly, worried about disturbing others. To stay healthy, they benefit from safe ways to share these feelings—talking to a friend, writing in a journal, or seeking a counselor if needed.

Recognizing Mood Changes

Because Libras prefer everything to run smoothly, they might ignore small signs that they are feeling out of sorts. For instance, they might skip lunch to keep working or avoid a conflict by staying silent. Over time, these small things can add up, leading to irritability or resentment. A healthy Libra notices these early clues—like tension in the shoulders or a nagging feeling of unease—and takes steps to address them rather than letting them grow.

Physical Health Routines

Physical well-being also matters. A balanced diet can make a difference for Libras, who may feel sluggish if they eat too many heavy foods. Simple, varied meals with fruits, vegetables, proteins, and whole grains can keep their energy steady. Staying hydrated is another key habit. Libras might keep a water bottle close by or track their intake if they realize they often forget to drink enough.

Gentle Exercise

Libras who want to maintain fitness often pick mild or moderate workouts. They could try yoga, light jogging, swimming, or dance workouts. Some might enjoy nature walks in scenic areas, letting them combine fresh air with gentle movement. A Libra might not aim for very intense sessions, but consistency helps keep them energized. They might schedule these workouts in a way that does not feel overwhelming—maybe a short walk each day or a longer session a few times a week.

Sleep Habits

Getting enough rest is crucial for Libras. When they are tired, they can lose their usual calm. They might become short-tempered or moody. Building a regular bedtime can help: turning off bright screens, dimming the lights, and doing something relaxing—like reading a simple book or listening to calm music—before sleep. If racing thoughts keep a Libra awake, a short breathing exercise or a guided relaxation app might assist in settling their mind.

Social Well-Being

Relationships are important for Libras. They often feel best when they share a kind word or a friendly exchange with those around them. This can be family, friends, or even kind strangers. Spending time with others can boost a Libra's mood, but they must also watch that they do not spend all their energy trying to please everyone. Finding a balance between social time and personal downtime is key.

Setting Boundaries

Because Libras dislike letting people down, they might say "yes" to requests or invitations even if they are already busy. Overloading themselves can lead to burnout. Learning to say "I'm sorry, but I can't this time" can protect their health. They should remind themselves that declining a request does not mean they are uncaring. It can, in fact, preserve enough energy to be truly helpful in the areas where they can give their best.

Calming the Mind

Libras may enjoy quiet moments to think. They might find that a few minutes of slow breathing before bed or after waking up brings mental clarity. Visualizing calm scenes—like a peaceful garden or a gentle coastline—can soothe them if they feel anxious. Some Libras might explore mindfulness practices, noticing each breath or each sensation in their body. This trains them to catch stress signals early.

Managing Stress at Work or School

In busy settings, Libras can feel pressure if they sense tension or deadlines piling up. They might help calm the environment by stepping aside to organize tasks. Writing a quick to-do list and assigning realistic time blocks can reduce worry. If a coworker or classmate is upset, a Libra might lend an ear—but they should avoid taking on everyone's burdens. Stress management includes drawing a line when things become too much.

Nutrition and Snacking

Some Libras cope with stress by reaching for sweet or salty snacks. While a small treat can be comforting, too much can lead to a cycle of sugar highs and crashes. Maintaining a balanced approach—perhaps keeping fruit or nuts handy—can help keep energy steady. Libras might also enjoy the ritual of preparing a small, healthy snack in a pleasing way, like slicing fruit neatly on a colorful plate, which feeds their sense of calm.

Creating a Peaceful Environment

The physical space around a Libra can impact their well-being. A cluttered or messy area might make them feel uneasy. Keeping their home or work desk relatively tidy can bring a subtle sense of order. This does not mean the place must be perfect, but a little organization helps Libras feel less stressed. Some enjoy adding soft lighting or gentle scents—like lavender—to encourage a relaxing mood.

Positive Self-Talk

Libras may be kind to others yet harsh on themselves if they make mistakes. They might think, "I should have done that better," or "Why am I so unsure?" Over time, such negative self-talk can harm well-being. Learning to speak kindly to themselves—like saying, "I'm doing my best and learning" or "It's okay to take time to decide"—can boost self-esteem. This gentle approach acknowledges imperfection without creating guilt.

Healthy Communication

Emotional health often depends on how people talk about problems. Libras might worry that being direct will cause arguments. But bottling up concerns can lead to bigger conflicts later. Practicing calm, honest talks—such as saying, "I feel left out when decisions are made without me"—can help others understand them better. This approach preserves Libra's polite tone while ensuring their feelings are heard.

Avoiding Passive Responses

Sometimes Libras might avoid confrontation so much that they agree to things they secretly dislike. This can create hidden stress, as they carry frustration inside. A healthier route is a balanced expression of needs. Saying, "I understand your plan, but I have a different view. Can we find a middle ground?" can keep the conversation respectful while also protecting the Libra's well-being. Over time, this skill helps them avoid regrets or resentments.

Time Management

A packed schedule can overwhelm Libras, especially if they want every activity to be carried out nicely. To stay well, they can plan breaks between tasks or keep the weekend partly free. This gives them space to unwind or handle unexpected chores. If a Libra tries to be busy nonstop, their mood can suffer, and they might become less patient or caring. Remembering to leave gaps in the calendar helps them maintain a friendly spirit.

Supportive Friendships

Friendships play a big role in Libra's emotional health. They like friends who appreciate their fairness and gentle approach. If a friend constantly pushes them around or scoffs at their polite style, the Libra could feel drained. Selecting friends who respect boundaries and value open communication can improve emotional security. Over time, these positive ties help a Libra face challenges with confidence.

Problem-Solving Approach

When difficulties arise, Libras often try to weigh the pros and cons. If used wisely, this method can lead to balanced solutions. However, if a problem is urgent, endless deliberation might add pressure. Knowing when to act—and trusting that they have done enough thinking—can reduce anxiety. Sometimes, taking small steps toward a solution is better than waiting for the perfect plan.

Relaxation Techniques

Libras may want to keep a handful of easy relaxation techniques in their toolkit. This could include:

Deep belly breathing: Inhale slowly, filling the abdomen, then exhale fully.

Progressive muscle relaxation: Tense and release different muscle groups, from toes to shoulders.

Gentle stretches: A few yoga-inspired movements can loosen stiff muscles.

Listening to soft music: Particularly tunes with soothing melodies, which match Libra's taste for harmony.

These small actions can calm a Libra's mind if they feel stress rising.

Balancing Others' Needs with Their Own

Libras often look after other people's comfort, which is kind, but they must remember their own well-being too. If they notice they always cancel their personal plans to help someone else, it might be time to reset boundaries. Self-care is not selfish; it keeps a Libra's energy strong so they can continue to be supportive in a healthy way.

Positive Relationships

In close relationships, Libras might strive to make sure each person feels appreciated. They can do small gestures like cooking a nice meal or writing kind words. This fosters a pleasant environment for both sides. However, if the Libra's partner or friend never reciprocates, the Libra can feel worn out. Recognizing the need for fairness, Libras might calmly talk about how to share support so that the relationship remains balanced.

Handling Conflict Constructively

Conflict is sometimes unavoidable. Libras who do not want chaos might still need to address issues. Approaching a dispute with calm language, like "I want to understand your view, and here's what I feel," can prevent shouting matches. By focusing on facts and feelings in a level-headed way, Libras preserve harmony while tackling problems head-on. This approach can be healthier than avoiding conflict until resentments grow large.

Mood Tracking

One practical step for well-being is to keep a simple mood log. A Libra can jot down how they felt each day—happy, stressed, neutral—and note any triggers. Over weeks or months, patterns might emerge. Maybe they see they are often tense on Mondays after weekend chores pile up, or they feel sad on days when they skip lunch. With this insight, they can adjust habits or schedules to minimize triggers and build positive routines.

Professional Help

If anxiety or sadness becomes too much to handle, Libras should not hesitate to seek professional help. A therapist or counselor can offer strategies to manage emotions, set boundaries, or handle conflicts. Libras might appreciate the gentle, step-by-step advice that counseling can provide. This outside perspective can help them see that their well-being deserves as much care as the well-being of the people around them.

Healthy Boundaries in Technology

Many Libras like social connections online, but too much screen time can interrupt mental rest. They might find themselves scrolling late into the night, comparing their life to others. Setting boundaries—like logging off devices an hour before sleep—can improve rest and mental calm. Libras can also limit notifications to avoid constant interruptions that raise stress.

Spiritual or Philosophical Interests

Some Libras gain peace from exploring spiritual practices or philosophical ideas. This might include reading about moral teachings, meditating in a group, or finding meaning in nature. These pursuits can offer comfort, a sense of belonging, and moral guidance. As long as the Libra chooses a path that aligns with their values and does not harm them or others, it can be a positive source of well-being.

Work-Life Balance

A Libra who works long hours without pause might see their polite manner slip away due to sheer exhaustion. Keeping a work-life balance can involve negotiating workload, using vacation days, or communicating with bosses about realistic deadlines. If the job environment is very tense, they might look for ways to improve it—perhaps starting a calm, respectful tone in team meetings or suggesting fair solutions to common problems.

Meaningful Leisure

Leisure time that aligns with a Libra's personal values can recharge them. This may be reading poetry, creating art, or volunteering in the community. Engaging in tasks that bring a sense of contribution and joy helps them feel fulfilled. If free time is spent on activities that do not match their inner desires, they might feel empty afterward. Finding truly meaningful leisure keeps Libras from emotional burnout.

Self-Expression

Self-expression can be a big part of a Libra's mental well-being. Whether it is painting, writing, or playing an instrument, these channels let them process their inner world. Expressing themselves might also mean talking about daily events with someone who listens carefully. A supportive friend or family member can be an important part of the Libra's emotional toolkit.

Apologizing and Forgiving

Because Libras value peace, they often do not like holding grudges. If they offend someone or make a mistake, a sincere apology can help them restore harmony quickly and free them from guilt. Likewise, they might forgive others more readily than some signs, as they prefer to move forward. This can aid mental health by removing lingering resentment. However, Libras must still set limits with those who repeatedly treat them poorly.

Regular Check-Ins

Once in a while, a Libra might pause and ask themselves, "How am I feeling physically, emotionally, and mentally?" If the answer reveals stress, body aches, or sadness, they can plan steps to address it. That might be a day off, a visit with a loved one, a simpler meal plan, or even an appointment with a doctor. Making these check-ins a habit ensures little issues do not snowball into bigger ones.

Nature and Fresh Air

Spending time outside can greatly help a Libra's sense of calm. A stroll in a park, sitting by a lake, or simply watching the sky can clear their mind. The natural world often displays a soothing harmony—leaves rustling softly, water gently moving—which matches a Libra's preference for subtle order. Regularly enjoying nature can ease mental fatigue.

Handling Criticism

Libras want to please, so criticism can sting. If a Libra receives harsh feedback, they might brood over it or worry they have upset someone. A healthier response is to look at the critique fairly: Is it accurate? Could it help them improve? Or is it delivered in a rude way? Filtering comments through a balanced lens can keep them from getting too upset. If the feedback is valid, they can adapt. If it is spiteful, they can let it go.

Celebrating Small Wins

Libras do not have to hold grand events for achievements, but acknowledging small wins can boost morale. A short note in a journal—"I handled that meeting calmly"—or sharing with a friend, "I finished a tough task!" can reinforce a sense of progress. This mindful approach to personal success helps them appreciate the good moments, especially if they tend to focus on others more than themselves.

Speaking Up Early

In group settings, if a Libra has an idea or concern, it helps to voice it sooner rather than later. Waiting too long might lead to confusion or a last-minute scramble. Communicating needs and insights at the right time can reduce stress for everyone, including the Libra. This also shows self-respect, a key part of feeling well.

Financial Well-Being

Financial stress can hurt overall health. Libras might prefer to avoid big money disputes, but ignoring bills or overspending on pretty things can cause trouble later. Keeping a simple budget—income versus expenses—helps them stay calm. If money concerns arise, a Libra might talk to a financial adviser or a trusted friend for tips on managing funds in a balanced way.

Gratitude and Reflection

Pausing to note what they are thankful for, even if it is just one positive moment a day, can shift a Libra's outlook. They might realize they have supportive friends, enough resources to meet basic needs, or small joys like a lovely sunset. This practice of reflection can anchor them when life feels rushed. It reminds them that not everything is a problem to solve; many things are already going well.

Adapting Over Time

As a Libra grows older, their well-being needs might shift. A younger Libra could focus on balancing schoolwork and friendships, while an older Libra might care more about stable finances or comfortable routines. The Libra's sense of balance remains, but the details change. Adapting to new life phases—like starting a family, changing jobs, or retiring—means revising self-care strategies to fit fresh circumstances.

Avoiding Guilt

Some Libras feel guilty when they cannot please everyone or if they must say no. They might worry they are being selfish. However, self-care is crucial. A Libra who constantly puts others first can end up resentful or exhausted. Understanding that guilt is just a passing feeling and does not reflect wrongdoing can help them do what is right for their own health.

CHAPTER 17: LIBRA IN THE ZODIAC PATTERN

When people discuss the zodiac, they are talking about a circle divided into twelve segments, each linked to a specific time of the year. Libra is the seventh sign in this arrangement, nestled between Virgo and Scorpio. This particular position can have meaning for those who study patterns in astrology. In this chapter, we will explore how Libra fits into the overall sequence of signs and what that might suggest about Libra's role among the twelve. We will look at how Libra's time of year connects to certain seasonal shifts, how air sign traits may align with the bigger zodiac story, and why Libra's balanced nature can stand out against the backdrop of other signs.

A Quick Overview of the Zodiac Wheel

The zodiac wheel is typically presented in a circle, starting at Aries (the first sign) and moving in order: Taurus, Gemini, Cancer, Leo, Virgo, Libra, Scorpio, Sagittarius, Capricorn, Aquarius, Pisces, then back around to Aries. Each sign covers roughly a month's time (though not aligning exactly with calendar months). Libra's traditional period spans from around September 23 to around October 22, though exact dates can shift slightly year by year.

Since Libra is the seventh sign, it is just past the halfway mark of the zodiac year. Some think of the first six signs (Aries through Virgo) as focusing more on personal development, while the latter six (Libra through Pisces) lean more toward social, spiritual, or communal concerns. Libra's place at the start of that second half suggests a pivot from self-focused themes to more group-oriented or relational themes. This idea is not absolute, but many astrologers keep it in mind when describing each sign's overall focus.

Seasonal Context of Libra

In many parts of the Northern Hemisphere, Libra's time of year corresponds to early or mid-autumn. The intense heat of summer is usually fading, and nature often shows changes like leaves turning colors. Meanwhile, in the Southern Hemisphere, Libra occurs in early or mid-spring, with plants blooming. Either way, it can be a season of transition. People in the Northern Hemisphere might sense days becoming shorter and nights growing cooler, while those in the Southern Hemisphere might see the world warming up and coming to life.

For those linking Libra to the Northern Hemisphere's autumn, there is a notable event called the autumnal equinox (around September 22 or 23). It marks a point in the year when day and night are close to equal lengths. Because Libra is symbolized by the scales—an instrument of balance—some see a direct link: the equinox itself is a balance of light and darkness. This lines up with Libra's reputation as the sign of harmony. While not everyone uses these seasonal cues to interpret astrology, it can add meaning to Libra's identity as a sign that seeks evenness in all things.

Position Between Virgo and Scorpio

Libra sits right after Virgo. Virgo is often described as practical, detail-oriented, and helpful. It tends to focus on improvement and efficiency. Then we have Libra, which looks outward a bit more, focusing on relationships and fairness among people. After Libra comes Scorpio, known for depth, intensity, and probing emotional honesty.

Some astrologers say this sequence—Virgo, Libra, Scorpio—can show a process: first a focus on careful analysis or refinement (Virgo), then a quest for balanced social ties or fairness (Libra), and finally a plunge into deeper emotional or transformative experiences (Scorpio). Libra's place in the middle can act as a bridge between the more modest, service-oriented themes of Virgo and the more intense, transformative themes of Scorpio.

Modalities: Cardinal, Fixed, and Mutable

In astrology, each of the twelve signs also belongs to one of three categories, called modalities: cardinal, fixed, or mutable. These three qualities repeat four times around the circle. Libra is a cardinal sign, along with Aries, Cancer, and Capricorn. Cardinal signs are often seen as initiators or leaders. They mark the start of each season in many traditional frameworks:

Aries is linked to the start of spring (in the Northern Hemisphere).

Cancer is linked to the start of summer.

Libra is linked to the start of autumn.

Capricorn is linked to the start of winter.

As a cardinal sign, Libra can show leadership by directing group discussions, bringing fresh perspectives, or sparking cooperation. While Libra might not be as overtly forceful as Aries, it still exhibits a motivational spark: it wants to push people toward harmony, fairness, and better relationships. This cardinal energy means Libras often begin new social or creative ventures, even if they sometimes hesitate when finalizing certain personal decisions.

Elements: Fire, Earth, Air, and Water

Each sign also corresponds to one of four elements: fire, earth, air, or water. Libra is an air sign, along with Gemini and Aquarius. The air element is associated with thinking, communication, and ideas. Air signs often approach life by analyzing possibilities or forming connections between people and concepts.

As the middle air sign (in zodiac order, it comes after Gemini and before Aquarius), Libra can represent a balanced form of communication, as opposed to Gemini's more playful curiosity or Aquarius's more futuristic outlook. Libra's air nature is social, focusing on bridging minds and ensuring conversation flows smoothly. This emphasis on social harmony sets Libra apart from other cardinal signs: while Aries might push a personal agenda, Libra wants to consider everyone's stance, upholding fairness.

Balancing Aries (the Opposite Sign)

Each sign has an opposite sign across the zodiac wheel. For Libra, that opposite is Aries. Aries is the first sign in the zodiac, known for independence, directness, and a "go-getter" style. Libra, by contrast, emphasizes working together and seeking shared solutions. Observers note that the Aries-Libra axis represents the balance between self and partnership. Aries focuses on "me," while Libra looks at "we."

This duality does not mean Libras ignore themselves, nor that Aries folks do not care about others. But it highlights that each sign can provide the quality that the other might lack. Aries can remind Libra to be more decisive and assert personal desires; Libra can teach Aries to be more considerate and weigh others' views.

Connections to Other Cardinal Signs

The other cardinal signs are Cancer and Capricorn, each starting their respective seasons. Libra, Cancer, and Capricorn share a proactive spirit—they generally do not just wait for things to happen. But they express this drive differently. Cancer's cardinal nature emerges in emotional nurturing or protecting loved ones. Capricorn's cardinal nature shows up in ambition, organization, or climbing professional heights. Libra's cardinal trait shines in social leadership and the creation of balanced group dynamics.

When these cardinal signs clash or cooperate, interesting outcomes can arise. Libra's calm approach can smooth over Cancer's mood swings or Capricorn's sometimes stern attitudes. Meanwhile, those signs can push Libra to be more decisive or handle emotions in a deeper way. Understanding these differences helps clarify how Libra's cardinal side is special—more about forging harmony than about building personal achievements (Capricorn) or emotional security (Cancer).

Transiting Planets Through Libra

In astrology, planets move through each sign of the zodiac over time. When a planet is said to be "in Libra," some say the qualities of Libra might color the planet's energy. For instance, if the planet of communication (Mercury) transits Libra, people might collectively focus on more polite or balanced dialogue for that period, at least according to those who follow these ideas.

Similarly, if the sun is in Libra (roughly late September to late October), many claim that society as a whole might place extra importance on fairness or social connections. Whether a person fully believes these patterns or not, it is interesting to notice that many events or discussions about equality happen around this time in some regions, possibly reflecting these ideas in action.

Historical and Mythological Roots

The zodiac pattern has roots in ancient civilizations, from Mesopotamia to Greece and Rome. Libra, as we discussed, was once possibly connected to the claws of the Scorpion before becoming its own constellation of the scales. Over time, the scales idea stuck, particularly in Greco-Roman contexts, tying Libra to themes of justice.

It is also said that around Libra season (particularly near the equinox), certain festivals in the ancient world honored balance or marked transitions in the agricultural cycle. While the precise details vary by culture, many found significance in that moment of near-equal day and night, reinforcing the concept of evenness. The zodiac pattern as a whole was used for calendars and spiritual or philosophical reflection, and Libra's spot after Virgo and before Scorpio fit smoothly into an ever-turning cycle of growth, harvest, reflection, and transformation.

The Shift from Virgo to Libra

Virgo's symbol is often the maiden, representing purity, details, or harvest time. Then we enter Libra, which focuses on cooperative partnerships. This shift can be interpreted as moving from personal improvement (Virgo's quest for perfection) to interpersonal improvement (Libra's quest for fair relationships). People who see an overall storyline in the zodiac might say that after perfecting the self, one is ready to form balanced relationships.

Another viewpoint is that Virgo sees the flaws in processes or systems and aims to fix them; Libra extends that to balancing how people relate to each other, ensuring that flaws in social or legal processes get resolved. Both signs care about what is "correct" or well-ordered, but Virgo focuses on practical details, while Libra focuses on the broader social or ethical picture.

Libra as a Midpoint Between Leo and Scorpio

If we zoom out a bit, Libra also sits between Leo (the fifth sign) and Scorpio (the eighth sign), with Virgo in between them. Some astrological thinkers group signs in sets of four or observe patterns that jump around the wheel. While that can get complicated, it can be interesting to note that Libra is the sign right after the final sign of the summer set (Leo, in the Northern Hemisphere) and just before the middle sign of autumn (Scorpio).

People sometimes see Leo's flamboyant expression as in need of a balancing calm. Virgo partly does that with modesty, and Libra continues it by focusing on outward harmony. Then Scorpio brings intense emotional depth. Each sign, in turn, modifies or balances out the extremes of the previous one. That is the essence of the zodiac pattern: constant shifts so that no single energy dominates for too long.

Lessons from Each Sign

The zodiac pattern can also be viewed as a learning process. Aries teaches about individual initiative, Taurus about stability, Gemini about curiosity, Cancer about care, Leo about confidence, Virgo about refinement, Libra about mutual respect, Scorpio about transformation, Sagittarius about adventure, Capricorn about discipline, Aquarius about innovation, and Pisces about empathy.

With Libra in the seventh slot, many say it offers the lesson of building fair relationships. In practical terms, it can mark a time or stage in life where you stop focusing on only your personal growth (as might be the case with the first six signs) and begin to include other people's needs and viewpoints. Whether or not this is taken literally, it offers a framework for thinking about each sign's symbolic function.

Libra's Role in Social Harmony

In the grand cycle, Libra often stands out as the diplomat. Where other signs might press forward with their own agendas, Libra tries to unify or compromise. This role can be tricky because it can lead to indecision or a fear of taking sides. Still, it is a vital function in group settings: someone has to step up and say, "Let's find common ground." In the zodiac pattern, Libra's presence reminds everyone that relationships require effort and fairness to flourish.

Comparisons With Other Air Signs

Gemini, Libra, and Aquarius each reflect air qualities in different ways. Gemini is the first air sign: flexible, curious, a bit scattered sometimes, focusing on collecting facts and chatting freely. Libra is the second air sign, often described as refined, seeking harmony in thought and manner, less scattered but still very much about communication.

Aquarius is the third air sign, known for more fixed ideas about society and progress. Libra's place in the middle might show it as a balancing point between the youthful, inquisitive nature of Gemini and the firmly principled nature of Aquarius.

This middle position can also mean Libra is less flighty than Gemini and less rigid than Aquarius, though that is not always true for every individual. It is more of a symbolic trait: Libra attempts to weigh ideas (fitting the scales symbol) rather than jumping from one idea to another (like Gemini) or holding one big idea above all else (like Aquarius).

Why the Scales?

We have mentioned that Libra is represented by the scales, and how this symbol is unique—most zodiac signs are animals or human figures, while Libra's is an object. This can imply an emphasis on a concept (justice, balance) rather than on a specific character or creature. It suggests that Libra's energy might be more about intangible ideals or principles, rather than personal attributes like courage (Aries, the ram) or nurturing (Cancer, the crab).

The scales are used for measuring weight and ensuring fair deals, pointing again to how Libra might help measure and balance the differences between people or ideas. In the zodiac pattern, it is a reminder that social fairness can be just as important as personal ambition, emotional nurturing, or creative expression.

Planetary Rulership

Another element of the zodiac pattern is that each sign is traditionally ruled by one or two planets. Libra is usually said to be ruled by Venus, the planet of love, beauty, and attraction. Taurus also shares this ruler, but Taurus is an earth sign, so it tends to apply Venus's traits to physical comfort and possessions. Libra, as an air sign, applies Venus's traits to relationships, conversation, and aesthetic expression.

Some speak of Libra as the "masculine" or extroverted expression of Venus, and Taurus as the "feminine" or introverted one. Libra's approach is more social and mental—valuing pleasant manners, elegant words, and balanced interpersonal ties. The zodiac pattern thus includes two signs ruled by Venus, but expressing that planet's themes in distinct ways.

Progression Through the Signs

One way to see the zodiac pattern is as a life story starting at Aries (birth or self-awareness) and ending at Pisces (transcendence or merging with the collective). Libra's role in that story is sometimes described as the stage where we learn to relate to another as an equal. The first six signs might focus on building an individual identity, while the latter six revolve around connecting that self to others and, eventually, to the broader universe.

This viewpoint suggests that Libra's main question is, "How do I find balance between me and you?" or "How do we share space and ideas fairly?" Achieving this can be complex, as people have different needs. Libra steps in to weigh those needs, bridging possible gaps. If a person is drawn to the zodiac as a symbolic narrative, Libra's spot can be seen as the turning point from personal growth to mutual understanding.

Eclipses and Libra

Sometimes eclipses (solar or lunar) occur in signs that lie opposite each other along the zodiac wheel. When eclipses happen in Libra or Aries, astrologers say that people may feel strong shifts related to self (Aries) versus partnership (Libra). Whether one believes this or not, it highlights another dimension of how Libra fits into the pattern: it stands at the cusp of big changes in how individuals approach relationships or conflicts.

Historically, cultures tracked eclipses and sometimes connected them with dramatic events. If an eclipse happened when the sun or moon was in Libra, it might have been seen as a sign of changes in alliances, treaties, or social structures. While modern science explains eclipses more precisely, the symbolic linking of these cosmic events with Libra's emphasis on fairness can still appear in some astrological circles.

Groupings and Triplicities

In traditional astrology, the twelve signs are also grouped by element (making four "triplicities"): fire, earth, air, and water. Since Libra belongs to the air triplicity, it forms a triangle with Gemini and Aquarius on the zodiac wheel. These triplicities can be used to interpret relationships between signs. Libra stands in harmonious aspect to Gemini and Aquarius if one uses certain astrological techniques. This suggests that air signs can collaborate or "get" each other more easily, at least in theory.

Additionally, the cardinal signs—Aries, Cancer, Libra, Capricorn—can form a cross shape on the zodiac wheel, marking the four main seasonal turning points (again, in the traditional Northern Hemisphere framework). This cardinal cross reveals a dynamic energy among these signs, each initiating changes in their own style.

Progressed Charts and Personal Growth

In more advanced astrological systems, a person's chart can "progress" over time, meaning that each day after birth might symbolize a year of life, shifting the positions of the sun, moon, and planets. If someone's sun was in Virgo when they were born, it might "progress" into Libra years later, which some see as bringing more Libra themes (focus on fairness, better diplomacy) to that person's life. This is another way the zodiac pattern influences how people interpret changes in character or perspective over time.

The Influence of Oppositions

We mentioned the Aries-Libra axis. But there are also other ways Libra might form an opposition in a person's chart, such as with planets in Aries or with the sign that squares Libra (Cancer or Capricorn). Oppositions in astrology are said to create tension or a need to balance two different sets of traits. If someone has a chart with many planets in Libra and many in Aries, they may feel pulled between personal drive and the need for cooperation. This can be a central theme in their life.

The zodiac pattern, then, is more than just a simple circle. It is a web of lines, angles, and relationships. Libra's presence in that web emphasizes bridging opposites, smoothing rough edges, and finding middle ground—some say it is like a cosmic negotiator.

Why Some Libras Feel "Different"

Not everyone who has a Libra sun sign fully relates to the typical Libra descriptions. This can happen if they have a cluster of planets in more intense signs (like Scorpio) or if their ascendant (rising sign) is quite strong. Still, the broad zodiac pattern underscores Libra's key place as a sign that addresses fairness in relationships. Even those Libras who act more withdrawn or emotional might still have that underlying wish for even-handed treatment.

Libra's Harmony in Society

On a larger scale, if one imagines the zodiac signs as stages of community development, Libra could represent the need for laws, social contracts, or polite norms that keep groups functioning. Aries might spark leadership or warfare, Taurus might bring resources, Gemini might spread information, and so on—until we reach Libra, which tries to ensure everyone is treated fairly within that growing community. This pattern can be extended to describe how societies evolve from raw beginnings (Aries) toward more structured relations (Capricorn) or even universal compassion (Pisces). Libra's spot in that evolution is all about forging respectful ties.

Differences in Tropical and Sidereal Astrology

It is worth noting that there are different zodiac systems, such as the tropical zodiac (common in Western astrology) and the sidereal zodiac (used in some Eastern traditions). They might not align exactly with the same star constellations due to shifts in Earth's axis over centuries. Thus, someone who is a Libra in tropical astrology might be a different sign in sidereal astrology. However, each system has its own internal logic, and Libra's symbolic place remains the same in the Western tropical pattern: the seventh sign, tied to balance and partnership.

Myths of Balanced Seasons

In older texts, people often connected the start of Libra season to a time of year when days and nights were roughly balanced. This can provide an intuitive sense that the cosmos is reflecting an even division—mirroring the idea of the scales. Even though the exact date of the equinox can shift, the symbolic link between Libra and the concept of equality in daylight is still strong in many astrological traditions.

Some legends or myths personify Libra as a judge or as a figure who stands at a cosmic gate, weighing each person's deeds. These myths can vary widely across cultures, but they reinforce the notion that Libra is about moral or social equilibrium.

Yearly Cycle of the Sun

The sun's apparent path around Earth (from our perspective) is what defines the zodiac. Each sign gets about a month of sun time, and during Libra's month, people in the Northern Hemisphere see the environment winding down from the peak of summer. Farmers might be harvesting crops, and communities might shift their daily rhythms. This is historically a period of reflection and organization for the colder months ahead. Libra's association with organizing, balancing resources, and ensuring fairness in sharing harvests or preparing for winter can be traced here too.

Meanwhile, in the Southern Hemisphere, Libra aligns with spring, a time of fresh growth and new blossoms. Even there, people might connect Libra with the idea of distributing resources fairly or planning events as weather becomes warmer. The core theme is still one of making sure everyone can flourish in a balanced way.

Influence on Personality

Of course, not everyone believes that the zodiac pattern affects personality. But for those who do, Libra's place means a person with a Libra sun (or other strong Libra influences) might be predisposed toward polite, well-structured interpersonal behavior. They might also find themselves dealing with a lot of real or symbolic balancing acts in life. For instance, they could be the one who mediates family arguments or organizes group activities.

The zodiac pattern might be seen more as an archetype or set of symbols rather than a literal cause. In that sense, Libra's spot among the twelve is a reminder that harmony and fairness are essential stages in any growth process—whether personal, social, or spiritual.

Progressive Steps: Aries to Libra

Let us briefly summarize the steps from Aries to Libra to see the storyline:

Aries: The birth of self, raw energy, "I am."

Taurus: Learning stability, gathering resources, "I have."

Gemini: Curiosity, communication, "I think."

Cancer: Emotional grounding, family ties, "I feel."

Leo: Self-expression, creativity, "I shine."

Virgo: Service, refinement, "I improve."

Libra: Partnership, fairness, "We balance."

Libra emerges after a person or community has established identity, resources, communication, emotional bonds, confidence, and practical skills. The next natural question is: "How do I share all this with another person in an equal way?" That is where Libra steps in.

Ties to the House System

In Western astrology, the zodiac signs and the astrological houses are two different concepts, but they can line up. Libra traditionally aligns with the seventh house of partnerships in the standard wheel. Whether or not a person's actual seventh house is in Libra depends on their birth time and place, but the idea stands: the seventh house deals with relationships, alliances, and sometimes open enemies. Placing Libra there symbolically underscores the sign's focus on how we connect with others—be it marriage, friendship, or formal agreements.

Global Variations

While Western astrology places Libra in this position, there are many other astrological or star-based systems around the world that interpret the sky differently. However, the concept of balance or scales is found in multiple cultures. For instance, the idea of measuring the soul, or justice, or cosmic equilibrium, shows up in various mythologies. This cross-cultural presence of scales as a symbol for fairness might hint that the themes we link to Libra are widely appreciated in human thought.

Even if other systems do not call it "Libra," they may still note a constellation or a time of year that deals with these ideas.

Libra's Relationship to the Eighth House (Scorpio's Domain)

Right after Libra in the standard house setup is the eighth house, often linked to Scorpio themes: shared resources, transformation, deep emotional processes. Some astrologers see it as a natural extension: once partnerships are formed in Libra, the next step is deeper merging in Scorpio (money, secrets, trust). If Libra is about the surface-level agreement—"Let's treat each other fairly"—Scorpio is about the hidden layers and what happens when you share your entire self, which can be intense. Libra's position in the zodiac pattern is thus the gateway to that deeper emotional world.

Polarity With Aries

Re-emphasizing the Aries-Libra opposition helps some folks better understand Libra's role: Aries leaps forward on its own, Libra steps back to see if others are included. Aries can be impatient, while Libra might be more measured. Aries fights for personal freedom, Libra negotiates for mutual benefit. Neither approach is "better"; both can be healthy or unhealthy depending on the situation. The zodiac pattern places them across from each other so that we might learn to integrate both sides over time.

Long-Term Progress

In a hypothetical narrative of personal evolution, a person might start as an Aries-like figure, discovering individuality. They gather lessons from each sign in turn. By the time they reach Libra's stage, they have hopefully built enough self-understanding that they can now form balanced, respectful connections. This cyclical pattern never truly ends—people can keep cycling through lessons all their lives. But Libra marks a key milestone: bridging the gap between the self and the other in a harmonious way.

How Libra Stands Out

Among the zodiac signs, Libra is unique in that it is represented by a non-human, non-animal symbol. Scorpio is the scorpion, Sagittarius is the archer (part human, part horse), Capricorn is the sea-goat, and so on. Libra's scales are purely symbolic, emphasizing an ideal. Some read this as meaning Libras might place strong importance on concepts, ethics, or ideals of justice, more so than purely instinctive or emotional drives. This can be both a strength (fair-mindedness) and a challenge (potential for overthinking or detachment from raw feelings).

Evolution Toward Scorpio

Once Libra's job of ensuring fairness in outward relationships is complete, the zodiac wheel moves to Scorpio, where transformation and deeper emotional truths come into play. The line between Libra and Scorpio can be tricky—some people born on the cusp might feel elements of both. But in the bigger zodiac pattern, we see a shift from polite, surface-level equilibrium to passionate, below-the-surface intensity. Libra tries to prevent conflict by reason; Scorpio might dive into conflict to uncover hidden truths. That is another reason the pattern is instructive: it shows how life experiences can move from gentler negotiation to confronting deeper issues.

Synergy With Other Signs

Libra forms "trines" with other air signs (Gemini and Aquarius), meaning angles of about 120 degrees in the zodiac circle, which are often seen as smooth or cooperative aspects. It also forms "squares" (about 90 degrees) with Cancer and Capricorn—both cardinal signs. Those squares can create friction that pushes Libras to act when they might otherwise stay neutral. Meanwhile, the conjunction with itself (planets in Libra) can amplify Libra's qualities. These relationships in the zodiac pattern underscore how no sign stands alone; each sign interacts in a geometry of angles that shape potential synergy or tension.

Planetary Cycles

Over the course of years, outer planets like Saturn or Jupiter might move through Libra and "test" or "expand" Libra's themes. For example, when Saturn transits Libra (which happened in 2009-2012 in Western astrology), some claimed it forced societies to examine fairness in laws, relationships, and contracts more strictly. Whether one believes that or not, it highlights how Libra's area of concern (justice, relationship structures) can become a focus during certain periods in the big cosmic cycles.

People who watch these cycles might notice patterns: during Jupiter in Libra, there could be an emphasis on diplomacy or forming alliances. During Saturn in Libra, a stricter or more realistic view of fairness might surface. Each time, the zodiac pattern is said to direct communal attention to Libra's domain.

Why the Zodiac Pattern Matters

For those who enjoy astrological symbolism, the zodiac pattern is like a map for both personal and collective growth. Each sign contributes a key concept or quality. Libra's concept is the bridging of differences and the creation of peaceful connections. By seeing how Libra fits into the circle—between Virgo's practicality and Scorpio's emotional intensity, opposite Aries's individual fire—people can grasp Libra's role more fully. It is the sign that stands for calm negotiation, measured decisions, and the desire to weigh each side fairly.

CHAPTER 18: LIBRA'S CONNECTIONS WITH OTHER SIGNS

One of the most frequent questions people ask in astrology is, "How does a Libra get along with each of the other signs?" While it is important to remember that every person is unique, many like to explore these broad patterns for fun or insight. In this chapter, we will look at how Libra might connect with Aries, Taurus, Gemini, Cancer, Leo, Virgo, Scorpio, Sagittarius, Capricorn, Aquarius, and Pisces. We will note the general pluses and potential hurdles, keeping in mind that real-life relationships depend on much more than sun signs alone.

Libra and Aries

- **Similarities**: Both are cardinal signs, so they share a proactive energy. They can spark each other into action. Aries respects Libra's willingness to weigh options (though Aries might find it slow sometimes), while Libra admires Aries's courage and decisiveness. They can be a power team if they pool their strengths.
- **Differences**: Aries is direct, impulsive, and strong-willed, whereas Libra is more diplomatic and cautious. Aries may see Libra as avoiding tough decisions, while Libra may see Aries as pushy. The best solution is for Aries to give Libra time to consider things, and for Libra to assert boundaries rather than always giving in. Over time, they can teach each other about self vs. partnership.

Libra and Taurus

- **Similarities**: Both signs are ruled by Venus in traditional astrology, so they share a love of beauty, comfort, and enjoyment. They might bond over music, art, good food, or decorating a pleasant home. Their calm dispositions can create a warm atmosphere.
- **Differences**: Taurus is a fixed earth sign, wanting stability and routine. Libra is an air sign, more open to discussion and shifting opinions. Taurus might find Libra too indecisive; Libra might find Taurus too stubborn. Still, they can get along if Taurus learns to bend a little, and Libra learns to stick to a choice rather than trying to keep changing the plan. Their shared love of comfort can smooth conflicts.

Libra and Gemini

- **Similarities**: Both are air signs, so communication often flows easily. They can talk for hours about ideas, people, or events. There is a natural mental connection, with Gemini's quick wit meeting Libra's thoughtful perspective. Socializing together can be fun, as both enjoy meeting people.
- **Differences**: Gemini is more restless and can jump from one idea to another quickly. Libra wants harmony and might get stressed if Gemini's scattered interests cause chaos. Meanwhile, Gemini might see Libra as too concerned with pleasing everyone. Overall, they can have a lively friendship or romance if they accept each other's mental pace. Libra can add structure to Gemini's spontaneity, and Gemini can help Libra lighten up.

Libra and Cancer

- **Similarities**: They are both cardinal signs, so they can start projects or shape environments. They also care about

relationships—Cancer nurtures loved ones, and Libra wants fairness in those relationships. At best, they can form a gentle, supportive bond.
- **Differences**: Cancer is a water sign, driven by emotion, while Libra is an air sign, driven by thought. Cancer might say Libra is too detached or logical, while Libra might feel Cancer's emotional swings are overwhelming. They need open communication: Libra learns to show genuine care for Cancer's feelings, and Cancer learns to trust Libra's attempt to keep things balanced rather than seeing it as cold. With patience, they can create a comforting environment.

Libra and Leo

- **Similarities**: Both can be social, enjoying gatherings and creative expression. Libra admires Leo's warmth and confidence, while Leo appreciates Libra's style and grace. They might bond over art, fashion, parties, or performances.
- **Differences**: Leo is a fire sign, eager for attention and praise. Libra can provide it, but might feel overshadowed if Leo demands the spotlight too often. Leo, in turn, might wish Libra were more decisive instead of trying to please everyone. Yet their combined charm can be quite magnetic. If they respect each other's roles—Leo as the vibrant performer, Libra as the refined coordinator—they can shine together.

Libra and Virgo

- **Similarities**: Both prefer neatness and can be detail-oriented in their own ways. Virgo organizes practical tasks; Libra organizes social or aesthetic matters. They might collaborate well on shared projects if they communicate clearly.
- **Differences**: Virgo (earth) focuses on practicalities, flaws, and improvements, while Libra (air) focuses on social grace and balanced ideas. Virgo might find Libra's need for social

acceptance shallow; Libra might find Virgo's constant critique draining. They can learn from each other if Virgo respects the value of diplomacy, and Libra appreciates honest feedback. A sense of mutual respect for each other's talents is key.

Libra and Libra

- **Similarities**: Two Libras together can create a polite, peaceful atmosphere. They might love the same arts, social events, or thoughtful discussions. Both aim for harmony, so they usually do not have explosive fights.
- **Differences**: Indecision can be a major issue if both hesitate to choose. They might spend ages asking, "What do you want to do?" "I don't know, what do you want to do?" Conflict can also be swept under the rug if neither wants to upset the other. To avoid stagnation, at least one Libra partner or friend must be willing to make firm choices. Overall, they can be a pleasant match, but they need to ensure real communication of personal needs.

Libra and Scorpio

- **Similarities**: Both signs follow each other in the zodiac, so there can be a sense of fascination. Libra is drawn to Scorpio's depth, while Scorpio appreciates Libra's charm. They can form a bond that balances surface grace with emotional intensity.
- **Differences**: Scorpio (water) dives into secrets and strong feelings, sometimes revealing a possessive or jealous streak. Libra wants peace and might avoid going that deep, fearing conflict or drama. Scorpio might see Libra as superficial if Libra refuses to confront hidden issues. Good communication is essential, where Libra bravely faces heavier emotions and Scorpio respects Libra's need for respectful

interactions. If they manage this, it can be an intriguing partnership.

Libra and Sagittarius

- **Similarities**: Both signs can be social, enjoy meeting people, and share a love of ideas. Sagittarius is a fire sign with an adventurous spark, which Libra often finds exciting. Libra's diplomatic style can help soften Sagittarius's bluntness, while Sagittarius's optimism can lift Libra's mood.
- **Differences**: Sagittarius can be restless, craving freedom and direct honesty, while Libra strives to maintain politeness and balance. Libra might see Sagittarius as too brash or inconsistent, and Sagittarius might think Libra is too worried about others' opinions. They can get along well if they allow each other space—Libra for decision-making, Sagittarius for exploration—and come together for lively discussions.

Libra and Capricorn

- **Similarities**: Both are cardinal signs, so they can start initiatives. They might cooperate on shared goals if they respect each other's methods. Libra sees the social or diplomatic path; Capricorn focuses on structure and long-term planning. Both can appreciate serious discussion if it is productive.
- **Differences**: Capricorn (earth) is practical, often businesslike, and can be cautious about emotions. Libra (air) is social, seeking harmony. Capricorn might consider Libra's social niceties frivolous, while Libra might feel Capricorn is too rigid or cold. If they focus on a common objective—like building a stable environment—they can combine Libra's people skills and Capricorn's discipline. They need open dialogue so that Capricorn does not steamroll Libra, and Libra does not hide real concerns behind politeness.

Libra and Aquarius

- **Similarities**: Both are air signs, so they share intellectual curiosity and value ideas. They enjoy conversation and might have many common interests, like humanitarian efforts or creative pursuits. Libra likes that Aquarius can see the big picture, and Aquarius appreciates that Libra tries to keep things fair.
- **Differences**: Aquarius is more independent and can be stubborn about personal beliefs. Libra may want more compromise or closeness than Aquarius is prepared to give. Aquarius might see Libra as too eager to fit in socially, while Libra might see Aquarius as too aloof. They can have a strong mental bond if they agree on fundamental values, and each respects the other's unique style. This pairing can create innovative projects and broad-minded discussions.

Libra and Pisces

- **Similarities**: Both can be gentle, caring signs. Pisces (water) is empathetic and imaginative, while Libra (air) is thoughtful and polite. They might share an interest in art, music, or spiritual concepts. They can create a nurturing environment, each wanting to avoid harsh conflict.
- **Differences**: Pisces is highly emotional and can be vague about practical matters. Libra is more structured in conversation but sometimes avoids deep emotional confrontation. Pisces might find Libra's logic a bit detached from feelings. Meanwhile, Libra could feel frustrated if Pisces is too dreamy or indirect. Despite that, they can connect on a soulful level if they allow each other room: Pisces to feel deeply, Libra to keep the peace. Communication must be open so they do not silently drift apart.

General Patterns for Libra Connections

Air Signs (Gemini, Libra, Aquarius): Communication flows; shared interests in ideas. Potential for strong mental bonds. Watch out for indecision or overthinking.

Fire Signs (Aries, Leo, Sagittarius): Excitement, action, and social fun. Potential for dynamic relationships. Watch out for differences in speed or directness.

Earth Signs (Taurus, Virgo, Capricorn): Balance can be found if they combine practicality (earth) with diplomacy (air). Watch out for friction between Libra's wish for social harmony and earth signs' focus on tangible results.

Water Signs (Cancer, Scorpio, Pisces): Emotional depth meets Libra's social grace. Potential for mutual support. Watch out for conflicts between logic and emotion.

Work Relationships vs. Romantic One

While we typically think of these compatibilities in romantic terms, they can also apply to friendships, family ties, or workplace teams. A Libra might collaborate well with an earth sign coworker who keeps projects grounded, while Libra handles negotiations. Alternatively, in a romantic setting, Libra might prefer the open conversation that air or fire signs provide. However, actual synergy depends on the entire birth chart, upbringing, communication skills, and personal choices.

Avoiding Stereotypes

Even though it is fun to explore these patterns, it is wise to avoid rigid stereotypes. A Libra may get along wonderfully with a Scorpio if both have learned to communicate, or they may clash with a Gemini if disagreements arise about how to handle daily issues. Sun signs alone do not predetermine fate. Instead, they offer glimpses into the styles each person might bring to a relationship, giving hints on how to handle differences more gracefully.

Libra's Strengths in Relationships

Across all sign pairings, Libra has certain traits that usually help:

Diplomacy: Libras try to phrase concerns kindly and find middle ground.

Empathy: They pay attention to others' feelings, aiming to keep them comfortable.

Aesthetic Sense: They can add beauty or a pleasant vibe to shared experiences.

Fairness: Libras genuinely want a solution that respects everyone's viewpoint, which can reduce conflict.

Potential Weaknesses to Manage
 Meanwhile, Libras might run into trouble if they:

Avoid Conflict Too Long: Sweeping issues under the rug leads to bigger blow-ups later.

Seem Indecisive: Partners or friends can get frustrated waiting for Libra to pick a path.

Over-Prioritize Approval: Striving to make everyone happy might cause Libras to neglect their own needs, leading to hidden resentment.

Tips for Libra in Relating to Each Sign

With **Aries**: Stand your ground politely, and admire their courage.

With **Taurus**: Embrace cozy activities, and compromise on routines vs. novelty.

With **Gemini**: Keep conversations light but focused, and accept changes in topic.

With **Cancer**: Show genuine care for emotional needs, and calmly address issues before they escalate.

With **Leo**: Let them shine, and gracefully speak up when you need to decide something.

With **Virgo**: Value their advice but request more gentle feedback if needed.

With **Libra** (another Libra): Avoid endless "You decide!" "No, you decide!" cycles by assigning tasks.

With **Scorpio**: Respect their depth, but kindly insist on open, respectful dialogue.

With **Sagittarius**: Explore fun outings, and discuss bigger life views. Give each other space.

With **Capricorn**: Align on goals, and let them see your logical side. Show them the importance of social niceties.

With **Aquarius**: Embrace shared ideals, and accept their independent streak.

With **Pisces**: Offer structure while appreciating their imaginative side, and talk out misunderstandings.

Elements and Modalities in Daily Interactions

Understanding that Libra is a cardinal air sign can help. Cardinal means Libras do not mind stepping forward to initiate a social plan or mediate a conflict. Air means they like to talk things out and keep interactions mentally stimulating. In relationships, these traits can be an asset or a stumbling block depending on the other sign's style. For instance, a fixed sign (like Taurus or Scorpio) might appreciate Libra's leadership at first but eventually clash if they see Libra's "leadership" as inconsistent. A mutable sign (like Gemini) might love how Libra leads them to new social circles but can get bored if everything becomes too polite and cautious.

Finding Compromise

The key theme for Libra in all pairings is compromise. Libras do well when both sides are willing to meet in the middle. If the other sign is highly rigid or extremely impulsive, Libra might feel out of balance. However, Libra can also adapt or gently guide the other person toward a fair compromise. This skill can hold relationships together where otherwise they might break.

Deeper Emotional Bonds

For deeper bonds, Libras often flourish with signs that value conversation, respect boundaries, and appreciate aesthetic or social harmony. This can be a Gemini who loves exchanging ideas, a Leo who enjoys living life with flair but can be generous, or an Aquarius who shares intellectual curiosity. But that does not exclude the other signs; it just means more effort might be needed in bridging differences. In fact, a Libra-Scorpio bond, while challenging, can be quite strong once mutual trust is established.

Handling Criticism from Other Signs

Some signs, like Virgo or Capricorn, might deliver blunt or harsh critiques. Libra can respond by calmly stating how it feels. For example, "I hear your concern, but can we phrase it more kindly?" This invites the other sign to see Libra's perspective. If the other sign refuses to adjust, Libra must decide if the relationship is still healthy. This underscores how Libra's desire for politeness should not translate into tolerating disrespect.

Encouraging Others

Libras often excel at encouraging friends or partners. They might say, "I believe in your talent," or "Your idea deserves a chance." Fire signs enjoy this applause, water signs feel emotionally supported, earth signs appreciate the warm acceptance, and air signs like the mental boost. As long as Libra's encouragement is genuine, it can strengthen bonds. Just beware of empty flattery, as some signs (like Scorpio or Capricorn) might see it as insincere.

Romantic Chemistry

In romantic contexts, Libras typically look for someone who values sharing. They might find strong chemistry with fire signs, which can ignite passion, or with air signs, which can spark mental connection. Yet, each match has its own flavor. A Libra-Taurus romance might be soft and sensual, a Libra-Scorpio one might be intense and transformative, a Libra-Capricorn one might be quietly stable with some tension over who leads. The possibilities are wide; it depends on how each partner handles the differences.

Addressing Emotional Depth

Some water signs (Cancer, Scorpio, Pisces) can challenge Libra to go beyond surface harmony and discuss deeper feelings. This can be good for Libra's growth, but also stressful if the water sign demands constant emotional engagement. Communication is crucial. Libra can learn to say, "I'm trying to understand your feelings, but I need some time to process." The water sign must appreciate that Libra is not ignoring them, just approaching the issue in a more measured way.

Social Scenes

Libras are often the ones planning get-togethers with friends. They might coordinate events or outings, wanting everyone to mingle happily. Signs like Leo, Sagittarius, and Aquarius often respond well to these social plans. However, a more introverted sign, like Virgo or Cancer, might feel overwhelmed by big gatherings, needing smaller meet-ups. Libra can adapt by creating cozy gatherings where quieter friends do not feel lost. This balancing act is another example of how Libra tries to suit multiple personalities.

Conflict Resolution

No relationship is conflict-free. Libras typically try to solve arguments calmly and logically. This can work well with other air signs (who like talking) or with some earth signs that prefer practical solutions. Fire signs might get impatient if the talk goes in circles, while water signs might need more emotional empathy. Libra must learn to speak not just logically but also from the heart if the other sign is driven by feelings. Meanwhile, they can gently remind fire signs that stepping back to talk about the issue can lead to better outcomes than a quick blowup.

Friendships vs. Love

A certain sign combination might work better as friends than as romantic partners. For instance, Libra and Gemini can be great friends, but if romance is involved, they might need more grounding. Libra and Capricorn can be wonderful colleagues, supporting each other's ambitions, but romantic tension might arise if Capricorn is too controlling. The sun sign pairing is a broad backdrop, not a final verdict.

Long-Term Success Factors

For Libras, long-term relationship success often hinges on:

Ongoing respect: Partners or friends who belittle Libra's softness or courtesy can create resentment.

Shared interests or goals: A joint passion helps keep the bond alive.

Fair distribution of responsibilities: Libras dislike feeling one-sided burdens.

Open conflict resolution: Letting problems fester undermines harmony.

Emotional and mental compatibility: Even if they differ, each side must respect the other's approach.

Handling Different Temperaments

If Libra meets a sign that is very shy (like a cautious Cancer or a timid Pisces), Libra's social warmth can draw them out. But Libra must not push too hard, or the other sign may retreat further. If Libra meets a bold sign (like Aries or Leo), Libra can help refine that energy. The key is to notice how their styles blend or clash, then adapt communication or boundaries to create balance.

Workplace Connections

In a professional setting, Libras might pair well with detail-oriented signs like Virgo or Capricorn for tasks that require thoroughness, as Libra can handle negotiations or client relations while the other sign handles data or planning. With fire signs, Libra can form a dynamic marketing or creative team, blending flamboyance with diplomacy. The main pitfalls often come if the other sign is impatient or too controlling, while Libra tries to keep peace.

Dealing With Jealousy or Control

Certain signs—Scorpio, Taurus, Capricorn—can become possessive or controlling in relationships if they feel insecure. Libra must calmly but firmly set limits, saying something like, "I value our connection, but I also need personal freedom." If these signs see that Libra is not threatening their security, they usually relax. Libra can also reassure them with small gestures of loyalty, while refusing to let jealousy dominate.

Celebrating the Differences

One of the joys for Libra is noticing how each sign has its own strong points. Aries's bravery, Taurus's steadiness, Gemini's wit, Cancer's care, Leo's warmth, Virgo's diligence, Scorpio's depth, Sagittarius's optimism, Capricorn's ambition, Aquarius's innovation, Pisces's empathy—all can blend nicely with Libra's diplomacy. Each sign can add color to Libra's life. Libras rarely want a relationship that lacks variety, so these differences can be quite welcome.

Personal Experiences Vary

If a Libra grows up among a family dominated by, say, water signs, they might learn early how to handle emotions. That could shape them into a Libra who is more empathetic than the stereotype. If they have mostly fire sign friends, they might be bolder than typical Libras. This again proves that real relationships are about synergy, not just sun sign labels.

Caution About Generalizations

While we have listed common themes, it is important to repeat that sun sign compatibility is just one piece of a very big puzzle. Moon signs, ascendant signs, Venus placements, and personal experiences all matter. Two Libras might be completely different due to these nuances. The main point is that astrology can guide people to see potential friction or harmony, encouraging them to handle differences with insight.

How Libra Learns from Each Sign

A good exercise for Libras is to see what each sign might teach them. For example, Aries can teach decisiveness, Taurus can show stability, Gemini can show adaptability, Cancer can show emotional depth, Leo can show self-expression, Virgo can show thoroughness, Scorpio can show psychological insight, Sagittarius can show broad-mindedness, Capricorn can show discipline, Aquarius can show social vision, Pisces can show compassion. If a Libra is open-minded, they can pick up helpful qualities from each sign they interact with.

Avoiding People-Pleasing

Across all relationships, Libras risk losing themselves if they go too far in pleasing others. The solution is to keep open communication about their own needs. If a friend, partner, or coworker demands too much, Libra can politely say, "I appreciate your concerns, but I need time or space to handle my own matters." This self-care approach ensures a healthier bond with any sign.

Building Balanced Partnerships

Ultimately, Libra's gift is creating balanced partnerships. By blending energies—like a cardinal approach with a fixed sign's consistency or a water sign's depth—they can cultivate mutual respect. They often excel at bridging big personality gaps, using fairness and charm to hold things together. The best partners for Libra are those who respect both the Libra's calm reason and their own style, leading to a synergy that benefits everyone.

CHAPTER 19: LIBRA IN DIFFERENT SOCIETIES

When talking about Libra, many people focus on modern Western astrology. Yet, we can also look at how various societies, both past and present, might view balance, fairness, and harmonious relationships—the core ideas often linked to Libra. Although not all cultures use the same zodiac system, the concept of balance appears in countless places worldwide. In this chapter, we will see how Libra-like values show up in diverse customs, stories, and social rules. We will also look at how different historical periods have placed importance on fairness, sometimes connecting it to images like the scales.

Balance in Ancient Civilizations

Several early civilizations saw the universe as a place requiring balance among different forces. In ancient Mesopotamia—where some of the earliest star charts appeared—the idea of weighing right and wrong, or measuring goods fairly, was crucial to their legal systems. They recorded codes of law on stone pillars, indicating that fairness mattered in daily life. While they did not call it "Libra," the notion of measuring truth or goods with a scale was present.

Ancient Egypt also showed a deep belief in balance. Their concept of Ma'at was a principle that represented order, justice, and harmony. In the afterlife, the heart of a deceased person was said to be weighed against a feather to see if they lived a just life. Although that is not exactly the Western zodiac's Libra, it does mirror the idea of scales as a tool for measuring truth and morality.

Greece and Rome

The classical Greeks named the constellation of Libra, linking it to the scales. They also had stories about justice as a virtue. Their goddess of justice was often depicted holding scales, highlighting the theme of measuring right and wrong. In Rome, the scales symbol spread into the legal realm: Roman courts sometimes displayed an image of a figure with scales to show equal judgment.

Because the Roman Empire spanned large regions, the scales icon traveled far. Early astrologers like Ptolemy wrote about Libra as a sign associated with fairness and good relationships among people. By the time of the Roman Empire's peak, Libra was well known in the Western world. Even though daily life varied greatly across the empire, the idea that Libra signified just dealings and balanced exchanges fit with Roman law's emphasis on fairness for Roman citizens.

Medieval Europe

After the fall of Rome, Europe entered the medieval period. Astrology was still practiced by scholars, who often linked each zodiac sign to biblical or moral lessons. Libra, with its scales, was tied to ideas of fairness and moral balance. This symbolism showed up in illustrated manuscripts and stained-glass windows, sometimes with a figure holding balanced scales.

During these centuries, local laws, churches, and trades used scales to measure goods or to symbolize honesty in commerce. A merchant might have an emblem with a pair of scales to show they dealt fairly with customers. Though many common folk did not read detailed astrological texts, they knew the image of scales meant correct weighing and honest exchange—a practical echo of Libra's theme.

Renaissance and Enlightenment

In the Renaissance, interest in Greek and Roman knowledge came back strongly in Europe. Art and literature of that period often featured classical symbols, including the scales for justice and the zodiac images. Scholars studied ancient texts in Latin or Greek, refining astrological ideas. Libra was seen as a sign favoring reasoned dialogue and balanced government.

Thinkers of the Enlightenment era valued rational debate, fairness in law, and structured social agreements. While they did not all talk about Libra directly, their push for laws based on reason and fairness aligned with what we often call "Libra values." For instance, documents promoting human rights or fair trials remind us of the symbol of the scales: each side must be given equal weight before a judgment is made.

Non-Western Views

Although Libra is usually named in Western astrology, other cultures have zodiac-like systems. For instance, in Chinese astrology, the cycle is based on animals over a 12-year span, rather than monthly segments. That system does not directly label a sign "Libra." However, the idea of balance and harmony is deeply rooted in Chinese thought through the concept of yin and yang, which teaches the need for opposing forces to work together in harmony.

In parts of India, the Vedic astrology system differs from the Western one, using sidereal calculations. The sign that corresponds to Libra in Sanskrit is sometimes called Tula, which literally means "scale" or "balance." So, while the exact dates might shift from Western astrology, the symbol of a scale and the idea of fairness remain. This shows that the concept of balancing is universal, even if the details differ.

Modern Global Cultures

In today's world, people in many countries read "sun sign horoscopes" in newspapers or online. Libra typically shows up as "the scales," referencing fairness, partnership, and social grace. This Western zodiac has spread across the globe, sometimes blending with local beliefs. In some East Asian countries, folks might casually mention their Western zodiac sign alongside their Chinese zodiac animal, mixing the two systems.

While not everyone takes these horoscopes seriously, many still enjoy seeing if Libra's descriptions match their feelings. Social media often features memes about Libra's love for justice or style. Even people who do not follow astrology might smile when seeing the scales as a sign of "doing things equally."

Law and Justice Icons

In countless nations, the idea of justice is shown by a statue or figure holding scales. This figure might be called Lady Justice in Western art—often blindfolded to show impartiality. Even if the local culture is not heavily influenced by Western astrology, the scales remain a potent symbol. Courts around the world may have an emblem with scales to remind judges, lawyers, and citizens that fairness under the law is crucial.

While these legal images are not labeled "Libra," the link is plain: the scales measure each side equally, echoing the concept of balanced judgment. Some places also show a sword to represent the power to enforce decisions, but the scales remain the central icon for weighing arguments or evidence. That tradition runs parallel to the astrological notion that Libra stands for balanced solutions.

Festivals and Cultural Events

In certain regions, times that match the rough period of Libra (late September to late October in the Northern Hemisphere) might have events linked to harvest or reflection. People might gather produce from their fields, share it in markets, or prepare for colder months ahead. The sense of dividing resources fairly or ensuring each person in a community has enough resonates with the Libra theme.

In older pagan traditions, the equinox around the start of Libra season was sometimes marked with gratitude for the harvest and readiness for the shift in daylight. Though we avoid a specific word here, we can say folks recognized a moment of equal day and night. That sense of "equal hours of light and darkness" fits naturally with the idea of the scales. Over time, as societies modernized, these autumn traditions changed form, but the spirit of balance can still be found in local customs or family practices.

Gender Roles and Libra

Across many societies, fairness in relationships has also included discussions on how family roles are assigned. Libra's emphasis on partnership might resonate with movements that advocate for equal treatment of all genders. While these movements are not about astrology per se, the moral principle behind them—balance, mutual respect—can feel connected to Libra-like ideals.

For instance, in societies where tasks have traditionally been divided based on gender, some families are now splitting chores more evenly. People might not think about the zodiac, but this shift toward fairness at home lines up nicely with the Libra principle that each side should have equal input and respect. This is just one example of how the concept of fairness can show up in daily life.

Group Harmony in Asia

Some Asian cultures, like in Japan or Korea, place high value on social harmony and the idea of saving face, making sure no one feels publicly embarrassed. While that might not stem directly from "Libra" as an astrological sign, the practice of smoothing out social friction resonates with Libra's style. In these places, politeness, respect for others' opinions, and avoiding confrontations are common.

If a Libra traveler visits such societies, they might feel very comfortable with the shared focus on calm interactions. Conversely, if someone from these regions hears about Libra's traits—politeness, seeking harmony—they might find them familiar. This does not mean every person there is "Libra-like," of course, but it shows how certain cultural norms can be close to the sign's values.

South American and African Contexts

In many parts of Africa or South America, local traditions emphasize community support. Some indigenous groups highlight group decisions made by elders or council members, ensuring everyone's voice is heard. While they may not call it "Libra," that group-based approach to problem-solving lines up with Libra's idea of hearing both sides.

African customary law in certain regions can involve clan-based meetings where issues are discussed until a consensus is reached. The concept is to keep relationships stable, reflecting something akin to Libra's pursuit of harmony. Similarly, in parts of South America—especially among indigenous communities—communal living fosters fairness in resources and a balanced approach to disputes. These local customs, again, match the heart of Libra's symbolic meaning, even if astrology is not involved.

Urban vs. Rural Perspectives

In modern city life, dealing with crowds can lead to tension if people do not treat each other respectfully. Some city dwellers might adopt a fast-paced, individualistic style, while others try to keep a polite approach, giving each person room. Libra's emphasis on courtesy might feel more relevant in busy environments where crowding can cause conflicts. If we apply Libra's thinking, we aim to ensure sidewalks, roads, or public transport are used fairly and politely.

Rural communities, on the other hand, might rely on closer personal ties. Residents often share labor during harvest or building projects, dividing tasks so no one is overwhelmed. This sense of helping each other can align with Libra's fairness, with everyone giving and receiving support. Although not every rural area is peaceful, smaller communities often talk out problems in group meetings, following an approach that can echo Libra's search for balanced solutions.

Modern Media and Popular Culture

In many TV shows, comics, or movies, we see characters who behave in a "Libra-like" way: they are often mediators, seeking compromise among more extreme personalities. This is not limited to Western media. A comedic anime might feature a character who tries to keep the group calm, or a telenovela might have a kindhearted lawyer figure who stands up for justice. These roles mirror Libra's social concerns.

Even the word "Libra" might appear in brand names or local contexts. For instance, a bookstore or a coffee brand might choose "Scales" or "Libra" to imply balance or fairness. People around the world sometimes find the concept appealing when naming shops, groups, or products. It is another sign that the scales carry universal charm, whether or not folks realize it comes from an astrological tradition.

Internet Communities

Online, some communities emphasize respectful discussion. They might create guidelines to ensure each user's voice is heard. Moderators, in a way, act like Libras, stepping in to remove harmful or hateful content and keep dialogues balanced. This is not always successful, but the intention can be similar: keep the online space fair and safe for all.

Libra groups on social media often share memes about indecision, love for beauty, or a desire for calm relationships. People from different continents can connect over these jokes. They may also share experiences of how they handle conflicts or choose outfits. While it is playful, it shows how a Libra-like mindset can cross cultural boundaries when the fundamental ideas—politeness and equality—are widely understood.

East vs. West in Social Etiquette

Broadly, Western norms might push direct communication, while Eastern norms might encourage more indirect courtesy. Libra's approach of calm fairness can fit well in Eastern settings where face-saving is key, but it also can help in Western settings by smoothing direct remarks into polite ones. This is not a strict rule—there are many exceptions—but it highlights that no matter where you live, being considerate of others helps avoid fights.

Perhaps that is why the sign of Libra resonates with so many: we all know how good it feels when conflicts are settled calmly. Even societies with bold, straightforward speech patterns benefit from a Libra-style voice that says, "Let's see each side carefully before judging."

Shifts in Global Awareness

In the modern world, people pay greater attention to fairness on a global scale. Topics like climate justice, economic equality, or global health revolve around the idea that resources should be shared in a balanced way. Advocates may not mention Libra, but the principle is the same: we weigh the needs of different groups, trying to find a solution that respects everyone.

Global organizations sometimes hold summits where leaders from many nations discuss mutual concerns. These talks can be tense, but ideally, they aim for balanced agreements. The spirit of these negotiations—listening, compromising, and ensuring no one is left behind—reflects a Libra approach, though it can be hard to achieve in practice.

Artistic Expressions of Balance

Artistic traditions in places like China's ink paintings or Islamic geometric patterns show a strong sense of balance. Greek temples with symmetrical columns, Indian mandalas, or even African textiles can feature symmetrical designs that give a feeling of harmony. These expressions of balance are not always labeled "Libra," but they echo the theme of symmetry and measured structure.

Some modern artists incorporate scales directly into their work, referencing justice or equilibrium. Sculptors might create metal scales that shift with the wind, symbolizing how fairness can be delicate or easily tipped. Paintings may show a figure balancing two objects, hinting at decisions. Each culture can interpret these images in its own way, but the core message remains: balancing forces leads to harmony.

Examples of Balance in Community Traditions

In certain African communities, group members might meet under a "palaver tree" to discuss issues until a consensus is reached. In some Pacific Islander traditions, elders guide group decisions to maintain social equilibrium. Among Native American nations, there could be talking circles where each person speaks in turn, ensuring fairness in conversation.

All these traditions might never mention "Libra," yet they show how the concept of balanced speaking and listening is cherished. The scale is replaced by a circle or a tree, but the outcome is similar: weigh each voice, treat them equally, and find unity if possible. People can see that the message of Libra is bigger than just one zodiac system—it is part of the human desire for fairness.

Contemporary Movements

Modern activism for human rights, gender equality, or environmental protection often uses imagery of balanced scales to convey the idea that justice is needed. Campaign posters, logos, or protest art might display scales to show that some group feels weighed down or that they demand an equal share. Whether in North America, Asia, or Africa, the symbol translates across languages.

This broad acceptance of the scales demonstrates that while people might disagree on many things, most agree that justice and equality are good aims. Political parties, courts, and charities might use the scales in their emblems. Even large organizations like the United Nations highlight fairness among nations, echoing the same principle. Although not everyone connects this to astrology, the parallel with Libra is striking.

Small-Scale Social Customs

Beyond big movements, everyday life in many societies includes small customs of balance. For instance, a host might seat guests so no one feels left out, or split food portions so everyone gets an equal share. A teacher might take turns calling on students, ensuring each has a fair chance to speak. A friend group might rotate who picks the weekend activity, so decisions do not always fall on one person.

These simple acts might not carry an astrological label, but they are everyday examples of "Libra spirit": no one is overlooked, each voice is heard, and things are done evenly. Families often pass these habits down to children, teaching them to share, wait their turn, and treat others kindly. This teaching aligns with the global idea that fairness helps keep a community together.

Unexpected Places for Libra Traits

Sometimes, in places we might think are strict or harsh—like certain big-city markets or busy offices—people still find ways to maintain fairness. A manager might hold a weekly meeting to ensure each employee's suggestions are heard. A vendor might weigh produce carefully, double-checking that a shopper is not overcharged.

Even in high-stress industries, skilled leaders use balanced approaches to conflict. They might form committees or hold objective reviews, mirroring the concept of the scales. So while popular media might show cutthroat competition, many real-world workplaces quietly apply Libra-like reasoning: weigh the facts, treat employees fairly, and keep peace in the team.

Cultural Stories and Myths

Various folk tales mention a wise person who balances issues or helps villagers share resources equally. In West African tales, there might be a trickster character whose actions lead to lessons on fairness, even if done through pranks. In European fables, a king or judge might weigh a dispute in literal scales. In Middle Eastern stories, a caliph or wise figure uses reason to settle arguments justly.

These recurring story lines highlight how vital fairness is to communities. While each culture has unique legends, the moral often teaches that tipping the scale in your favor at someone else's expense leads to trouble. Instead, the hero or wise figure finds a balanced solution, reminiscent of Libra's approach.

Technology and Balanced Input

Today, technology can help or hinder fairness. On one hand, social media can lead to echo chambers and angry debates. On the other, online platforms can give equal voice to many people who otherwise would be unheard. Tools like community forums or volunteer-based websites rely on guidelines that resemble Libra's goal: let each side speak, moderate insults, and find a middle path.

In e-commerce, rating systems can reflect how well a seller deals with customers. The concept that each buyer's voice matters can create a fair marketplace. Even though this might not be labeled "Libra in technology," the underlying principle—balanced input from all—matches Libra's sense of justice. It shows how each new invention can be shaped by the timeless pursuit of harmony.

Global Celebrations of Justice

Certain international days or events focus on justice or fair treatment. People might hold parades, awareness campaigns, or public forums about equality and social well-being. The scale symbol or references to balanced fairness often appear on posters or websites.

Again, no single culture "owns" the scales. But the repeated appearance of this symbol, from ancient carved stones to modern digital banners, proves that the need for evenhandedness is widely shared. It also suggests that Libra's ideal can show itself in many forms, from quiet group meetings to large public gatherings.

Religious Parallels

In some religions, the concept of a final judgment or balancing of deeds is key. A deity or saint might weigh a person's actions, deciding their fate. This theological image sometimes includes literal scales in art or scripture. Even if the religion predates or stands apart from Western astrology, the scales are a common tool to show moral balance.

These parallels do not necessarily mean the religion follows Libra astrology, but they underline how humans around the world have used the scale as a sign of truth and justice for millennia. Whether it is an Egyptian heart against a feather, a Christian archangel holding scales, or a depiction in Islamic art of moral weighing, the motif recurs across faiths.

Honesty in Trade and Commerce

From the earliest markets to modern shops, honest merchants used fair scales to weigh grain, produce, or other goods. Cheating a customer by tipping the scale was seen as a crime. Laws or guild rules in medieval towns punished dishonest sellers severely. Today, electronic scales in supermarkets or digital check-out systems aim to keep that honesty.

Libra's symbol might not be printed on every scale, but the moral is the same: each buyer should receive exactly what they pay for. This practical matter of equal exchange in daily life parallels the bigger idea of giving each person their fair portion. In many societies, measuring goods correctly is not just a legal matter but also a point of personal pride among honest traders.

Family Dispute Mediation

In some local traditions, family elders or village chiefs help settle quarrels, dividing property or deciding on punishments. They rely on moral guidelines that say each side should be heard, each piece of evidence weighed. This stands out in rural communities lacking formal courts.

While the method might differ from Western legal systems, the principle is the same: look at each argument, find a balanced solution, and keep the peace. The wise elder might be like a human scale, listening to each side. This approach ensures that grudges do not linger, which is essential for close-knit communities. The elder is effectively a living symbol of Libra's balanced justice.

Contemporary Legal Innovations

Some countries try new strategies in law to ensure fairness, such as "restorative justice," where victims and offenders meet to talk out harm and find mutual healing. This approach aims to restore balance by letting each side explain their viewpoint and then agree on a fair resolution. Although it is not explicitly linked to Libra in official documents, the parallels are strong: conversation, fairness, and balanced outcomes.

Similarly, certain town hall models or citizen panels gather people from all backgrounds to discuss local issues. By giving equal time to every participant, these models reflect a Libra-like ethic that no voice should dominate. While results vary, the hope is that fair process leads to better social cohesion—again, aligning with Libra's key ideas.

Symbolic Observances

Around the world, many days highlight themes like equality, justice, or peaceful conflict resolution. For example, an international day dedicated to peace might use dove imagery, but it might also showcase the scales in promotional materials. Similarly, a day about legal rights might feature the scales as a reminder that the law is meant to serve everyone equally.

Such observances can unite people from different countries under the shared aim of fairness, bridging language or cultural barriers. The scale, recognized by children and adults alike, stands as a powerful sign that everyone deserves an equal voice.

Personal Identity and Online Expressions

With the internet, someone in Africa can connect with a Libra group from Europe, or a student in Brazil can chat with Libras in Canada. They swap stories of how they manage daily life: maybe they talk about each person getting an equal chance to pick a restaurant, or how they mediate spats among siblings. They might not realize these are universal issues, but once they share them, they see that fairness is a global desire.

Memes about Libra's indecision can resonate from the Philippines to Germany. People laugh about overthinking choices and wishing to keep everyone content. Even if cultural details differ, the comedic angle of trying to weigh two equally good (or bad) options is universal. This cross-border sharing blends astrology talk with simple human experiences, showing how Libra-like traits pop up everywhere.

Strengthening Bridges Between Cultures

One might say Libra's overarching lesson is to build understanding among different perspectives. In the modern world, cross-cultural dialogue is more frequent. Students study abroad, travelers see new lands, and businesses operate globally. Each time someone tries to mediate between two cultural norms, they act in a Libra-like way: searching for a fair middle path.

For instance, if a European company merges with an Asian firm, the new leadership might adapt rules to respect both sides. They weigh different working styles, meeting in the middle so that both employees and managers feel seen. This is not labeled "Libra," but it is exactly the same principle: treat each viewpoint fairly, find harmony.

Why Balance Attracts People

The scales carry a pleasing shape: two pans held level by a central beam. Whether physical or symbolic, they are easy to understand. Everyone can see if one side dips too low. The same goes for moral or social issues—if one group's voice is missing, the entire community can become lopsided. Many societies attempt to level this out through laws, moral codes, or daily courtesies. Libra-like behavior is simply how we fix that tilt.

This attraction to balance also shows in minimalistic designs, symmetrical buildings, or even balanced diets. Humans, in general, enjoy the comfort of even proportions. That is likely why Libra (the scales) has endured as a beloved zodiac symbol and a sign of fairness across cultures.

Education in Schools

Some school systems incorporate lessons on fairness from an early age. Children learn to share, to speak kindly, and to respect different opinions. They might read stories about wise kings or queens who weigh each side carefully. In older grades, they learn about the scales of justice, about equality under the law, or about historical figures who fought for balanced rights.

Teachers often mention that listening to classmates, waiting one's turn, and dividing tasks fairly is crucial for group projects. Students discover that respecting each other's voices leads to better results. While they do not call it "Libra thinking," the practice is much the same. This fosters a generation that grows up appreciating balanced solutions.

Modern Debates on Justice

Public discussions about how to share wealth, protect the planet, or ensure equal opportunities are ongoing in every country. People might hold diverse views, but they usually claim to seek a fair outcome. The challenge is deciding what "fair" looks like. Some want strict rules, others want more freedom, yet almost everyone says they want to avoid tipping the scales too far.

Libra's stance would be: gather facts, include all voices, aim for a balanced middle ground. In practice, finding that middle is tough. Still, many political or social thinkers speak about bridging divides—another sign that Libra's ideal continues to guide modern society, at least as a goal if not always as a reality.

Libra in Popular Horoscopes Worldwide

Whether you are in the United States, India, Australia, or Nigeria, you might see a newspaper column or website listing your Western zodiac. Libra's section might say things like "focus on balancing your personal and work life," or "maintain peace in relationships." People everywhere glance at these suggestions. They might ignore them or take them lightly, but the repeated theme remains: Libra, the sign that encourages calm, fairness, and courtesy.

Horoscopes in another language might adapt the style, but the message is the same: "You value peace," "You weigh things carefully," "You prefer polite interactions." People from different cultural backgrounds who identify as Libra often confirm that these qualities resonate, even if their daily life is shaped by their unique cultural norms.

Social Justice Programs

Universities or nonprofits sometimes launch projects aimed at fairness—equal access to education, unbiased hiring, or free legal help for those who cannot afford it. They do not have to mention astrology, but the underlying drive is that each person must be treated justly. In a sense, these programs enact Libra's dream on a broad scale: an environment where no one is neglected.

For example, a legal aid group might use the scales in their logo, symbolizing that they weigh each case fairly, no matter how rich or poor the client is. Or an educational charity might stress that all children deserve equal resources, a direct reflection of balancing the scale for underprivileged students. Though not created by "Libras only," these initiatives reflect universal principles often linked with the sign.

Challenges to Achieving Balance

Despite widespread agreement that fairness is good, many obstacles remain. Societies have inequalities in wealth, power, or status. Some people manipulate rules to tip the scale in their favor. Others might use strong tactics to silence certain voices. This shows that while Libra-like ideals are admired, they are not always practiced.

Nonetheless, the repeated push for reform, protest, or negotiation signals that the desire for balance never disappears. Folks keep returning to the idea that solutions should be fair, that no one side should control everything, and that disagreements should be talked through. This cyclical tension—struggling for fairness, losing it, then struggling again—has shaped history across all lands.

Libra's Global Reminder

Observing how the scales symbol and the idea of fairness appear in different places reveals that Libra-like values are part of being human. Whether it is a small village in Asia or a bustling city in Europe, whether it is an ancient temple or a modern courtroom, the concept of weighing two sides remains crucial.

Even though not everyone believes in astrology, the sign of Libra continues to inspire conversation about social grace and moral balance. In a busy world full of different opinions, Libra reminds us that respectful dialogue and equal consideration might help us find better paths together.

CHAPTER 20: KEY THOUGHTS ON LIBRA

After reading about so many angles of Libra—its history, personality traits, symbol, balance in emotions, and connections with other signs—you might wonder, "What is the main takeaway?" In this closing chapter, we will gather the core ideas about Libra to form a handy summary. We will also consider why these ideas still matter in daily life, regardless of whether one believes deeply in astrology or sees it as a fun guide. The sign of Libra can remind us of vital lessons about fairness, gentle communication, and sharing space with others in a balanced way.

Fairness as a Guiding Principle

Above all, Libra symbolizes an effort to treat people evenly. In many chapters, we saw how Libras want to ensure that no one's voice is ignored, no one is left out, and that decisions reflect a balanced view. This principle goes beyond star signs. It is a central human ideal—one that shapes laws, social customs, and personal friendships.

 Whether you are a Libra or not, thinking about fairness can help you reflect on how you share tasks at home, handle group projects at work or school, or settle conflicts with friends. Striving for a balanced approach often yields better relationships, fewer grudges, and a sense of cooperation. This main concept—justice and equilibrium—sits at Libra's heart.

Harmony in Conversations

Libra is known for polite communication, preferring diplomacy over direct confrontation. Some might see that as avoiding the hard truth, but it is actually about delivering the truth in a way that others can accept. When used wisely, this style smooths group activities. People feel heard rather than attacked.

We explored how Libras handle conflict: they might talk calmly, gather everyone's views, and propose a middle ground. That does not mean ignoring problems; it means dealing with them without causing extra hurt. Learning to speak with kindness, even when annoyed, can strengthen bonds. This is a skill many folks work on throughout life, whether or not they identify as Libra. So, Libra's approach can be a model: speak your truth, but do it gently.

Balancing Needs and Choices

Libra's scales also signify the act of weighing options. Many times, Libras are teased for being indecisive, because they pause to consider all angles. Yet, that pause can prevent rash decisions. Thinking before acting often leads to wiser outcomes. The challenge is to avoid overthinking to the point of inaction.

In daily routines—like picking what to eat or how to plan your day—a bit of Libra's method can help. You compare pros and cons, consider the impact on yourself and others, then decide. This is especially useful for group decisions, where each person's preference matters. By using a balanced approach, you show respect for everyone.

Cooperation in Work and Home

Libras often do well in teamwork. They try to see that tasks are shared, that each member of the group has a fair share, and that no one is overshadowed. At home, a Libra parent might teach children the value of taking turns. At work, a Libra manager might ensure each team member's ideas are included in a project. This fosters a sense of belonging.

Even if you are not a Libra, adopting that mindset can improve any group setting. Instead of pushing your own way, you ask, "What do others think? Can we find a compromise?" It may take more time than a simple top-down order, but it often leads to smoother cooperation, fewer resentments, and longer-lasting success.

Attention to Beauty and Aesthetics

Libras often express an eye for beauty, whether it is art, music, fashion, or interior design. They do not necessarily chase luxury; they just appreciate a setting that looks or feels harmonious. This attention to pleasant surroundings can lift spirits and make people more comfortable.

You do not have to be wealthy or fancy to adopt a bit of Libra's love for beauty. Sometimes it is as simple as keeping a tidy corner, placing a small plant on the table, or choosing color patterns that soothe you. This can influence mood, making spaces feel warmer and more welcoming to visitors. It is another way Libra's balanced approach shows up in real life: balancing function with an appealing touch.

Empathy and Emotional Calm

Many Libras are praised for empathy, noticing when someone is left out or upset. They are quick to include that person, offer a kind word, or mediate if there is conflict. This empathy is part of their desire to keep the social "scale" from tilting too far. If a friend is sad, the Libra might check in, or if a coworker is overshadowed, the Libra might invite them to speak.

Embracing empathy is valuable in any relationship. It involves listening, picking up cues, and responding with kindness. While some folks are naturally good at it, anyone can improve by paying attention. In a classroom, for instance, letting a quieter student share can build a sense of teamwork. Libra's example reminds us that empathy is not weakness; it is a strength that helps maintain harmony.

Challenges Libras Face Libra-like qualities can be positive, but they come with pitfalls:

- **Indecision**: Too much weighing can become hesitation. If you suspect you are stuck, set a deadline or trust your gut if the facts are equal.
- **Avoiding Conflict**: Peace is nice, but real problems must be addressed directly. If you push them aside, they might grow. Libras need to practice open talks, even about uncomfortable topics.
- **People-Pleasing**: Wanting everyone happy is kind, but you cannot please all sides at once. Libras should remember their own needs count too.
- **Over-Focus on Appearances**: Appreciation for beauty is fine, but it should not overshadow deeper matters. Real relationships require honesty beneath the surface.

Emotional Balance

Libras strive for emotional stability, but life is full of surprises. Unexpected events can shake anyone's calm. When that happens, a Libra might need coping methods: journaling, breathing exercises, or talking to someone they trust. All these strategies align with stepping back and regaining equilibrium.

Non-Libras can also benefit from these tools. Stresses at school, work, or home can make us feel off-balance. Taking a moment to reflect, then re-centering, helps us face challenges more calmly. Libra's approach shows that emotional balance is not about never being upset; it is about returning to an even state once the upset passes.

Importance of Listening

Since Libra focuses on fairness, listening is key. In arguments, a Libra might pause to let the other person speak fully. While some signs jump in with their viewpoints, Libra tries to absorb what the other side is saying first. This can build bridges instead of walls.

Real listening means not just waiting your turn but trying to understand. If more people did this, many personal and social tensions could ease. So, adopting Libra's listening style can help in everyday life: you might discover that someone's opinion, though different, has merit. You might find solutions you never considered. That is the essence of giving each voice a fair share.

Honoring Two Sides of a Conflict

The scale imagery suggests that every issue might have multiple valid angles. Libras do well when they accept that, yes, side A might have some correct points, and side B might have others. The trick is merging them or finding a middle path. This does not mean you cannot take a firm stand; it just means you consider each argument first.

In practice, this can lead to creative compromises. For example, if two friends disagree on what movie to watch, a Libra might propose a simple solution: pick a short film from each person's list, or alternate weeks. If two departments at work argue over budgets, a Libra manager might gather data to see a fair division.

These approaches avoid "one side wins, the other loses." While not every conflict can end in perfect compromise, aiming for partial balance still fosters mutual respect.

Growth Through Partnerships

Libra's place in the zodiac is linked to the notion that, after forming a strong sense of self (in earlier signs), we learn about the self through partnerships—be it friendship, romance, or collaboration. We grow when we share experiences with someone else.

Even if you are not a Libra, forming healthy partnerships can teach lessons you cannot learn alone. Each new person you connect with adds perspective to your life. If you keep an open mind and treat them fairly, your own understanding deepens. Libra's viewpoint says relationships are not just attachments; they can be mirrors showing who we are.

Libra at Work

In a job setting, Libras can shine in roles like negotiating, customer service, design, human resources, or leadership that requires diplomacy. Because they can see multiple sides, they help settle disputes and keep teams cooperating. They might also bring artistic flair if the work involves creating pleasant environments—such as event planning or interior design.

However, Libra employees may need help finishing tasks under pressure if they overthink. They might also dislike workplaces where harsh criticism is constant, as that undermines the calm they thrive on. Balancing constructive feedback with politeness can get the best from a Libra and from any team.

Libra in Family Life

As parents, Libras often encourage fairness among siblings: "Share your toys," "Let your sister choose this time." They try to keep home arguments from getting too heated. The flip side is that a Libra parent might find it hard to lay down firm rules if they want to stay liked by all. They should remember that children need clear guidelines, not just suggestions.

As siblings or children themselves, Libras might want everyone to get along, mediating squabbles. This is helpful but can be stressful if they feel responsible for others' moods. Learning to let family members sort some disputes out alone can relieve Libra from always stepping in. A healthy approach: help when needed, but do not carry the entire emotional load.

Libra in Friendships

A Libra friend is often the one who listens to your issues, tries to see your side, and offers gentle advice. They might text you, "How can I help?" or "Let's talk it out." In group settings, they ensure quiet pals get a chance to speak. Many people value such a friend.

However, Libras should also stand up for themselves if a friend becomes too demanding. Because Libras want harmony, they can slip into pleasing mode. Good friends appreciate the Libra's kindness but do not exploit it. True friendship means taking turns supporting each other. That principle also matches Libra's scales: the friendship needs to be even, with each side giving and receiving.

Relationship Advice from Libra

Communicate kindly: Even when upset, try to phrase your words so the other person can listen without feeling attacked.

Check for fairness: Are both partners sharing chores, emotional support, or bills equally, as best they can?

Listen carefully: Let your partner express feelings fully before jumping in. Summarize what you heard to show you understand.

Avoid silent resentment: Address problems early instead of burying them.

Celebrate small good moments: Notice little acts of kindness or understanding that keep the bond stable.

Dealing with Stress

Because Libras thrive on calm, stressful environments can drain them. School exams, office deadlines, or personal dramas all weigh on the mind. Having a plan to restore balance helps. That might involve a quick walk outdoors, a chat with a supportive friend, or a simple break to breathe and reorganize tasks.

Libras might also benefit from not taking on extra tasks just to please others. If they see a schedule is too packed, they can politely decline additional responsibilities. Setting boundaries is crucial for maintaining energy. This approach is relevant to everyone, but Libras in particular must watch out for the trap of over-commitment.

Libra's Role in a Group

Consider a typical group—maybe a classroom team, an office department, or a volunteer committee. Each member might have a style: one is bold (like Aries), another is detail-focused (like Virgo), another is emotional (like Cancer). The Libra person might be the diplomat who ensures no one is left out. They ask for each member's input, bridging differences.

Such roles are not officially assigned, but they emerge from personality. A Libra might naturally fill the mediator spot. If they do it well, the group stays smoother. If they let the role become overwhelming, they could feel stuck. The lesson: know your strengths but also share the load.

Libra's Relationship with Creativity

We mentioned that Libras can be drawn to art, music, or design. This is partly due to their Venus rulership, connecting them with beauty. They might write poems, decorate their rooms, or play melodic tunes. Creativity for a Libra is often about pleasing aesthetics or stirring calm moods.

You do not have to be an artist to enjoy creativity in a Libra-like way. Maybe you arrange the table nicely for dinner or pick complementary colors for your outfit. Each small act can reflect the same sense of proportion and harmony. In a bigger sense, creative expression can let Libras process their emotions in a balanced manner—turning stress into art or calm reflection.

Connecting Across Cultures

As we saw in the previous chapter, Libra-like values are found worldwide. People may not call it Libra, but fairness is universal. In daily life, you might meet folks from different backgrounds who also care about bridging differences. Libras can build friendships that cross cultural barriers by focusing on shared courtesy and equal dialogue.

If you move to a new country or city, these Libra traits can help: approach new people politely, try to see their perspective, avoid judging too quickly, and remain open to compromise. This fosters a welcoming environment, whether you are the newcomer or the local greeter.

Handling Criticism

Libras, wanting harmony, may get upset if others criticize them strongly. They might even blame themselves or become defensive. Learning to handle criticism without taking it too personally is important. A balanced approach is to see if the feedback holds useful points. If yes, adjust. If the tone is rude, calmly say you appreciate feedback but want it delivered with respect.

This logic-based response can keep tension low. Over time, Libras can build resilience. They remain polite but also stand firm if criticisms become unfair. That is another example of balancing: weigh the critique, accept what is valid, discard what is not.

Libra in Modern Technology

On social media, some Libras share their interest in style or post well-structured photos. Others run discussion groups, ensuring all members follow civil rules. They might help moderate online communities. This lines up with Libra's knack for managing social spaces.

Even in programming or technical fields, a Libra might excel by focusing on user experience or team communication, bridging "tech talk" and everyday language. They can use their balanced approach to ensure each stakeholder's needs are addressed. While it might not be about painting or chatting, it is still a form of fairness—everyone's viewpoint matters in building a good product.

Looking Forward

As life continues, Libras often refine their balancing act. Early in life, they might struggle to say "no" or to pick a path. With experience, they learn the difference between polite compromise and sacrificing their own well-being. They also gain confidence in deciding on a solution after careful thought.

Anyone can adopt that growth path. Maybe you used to either be too soft or too harsh. Over time, you realize you can be gentle yet firm. That is the sweet spot Libra aims for: kindly acknowledging others while not losing your own stance.

Libra's Symbolic Power

Sometimes people wear Libra necklaces or get tattoos of the scales to remind themselves of these ideals. Others might keep a small scale figure on a desk as a nod to fairness. These items do not magically solve problems, but they act as symbols, prompting a person to recall the values they wish to uphold—honesty, calmness, balance.

Symbols matter because they connect us to ideas quickly. Glancing at the scales can spark a moment of reflection: "Am I treating this situation fairly? Have I listened enough?" This small pause can alter choices, improving outcomes in personal or shared endeavors.

Finding a Personal Blend of Logic and Feeling

Libra is an air sign, leaning toward logical reasoning. But real fairness also requires empathy. You need to sense emotional undercurrents to truly weigh each side. A purely logical approach might ignore how strongly someone is hurting. Conversely, a purely emotional approach might ignore practical facts.

The best middle ground is to use both mind and heart. Libras do that well when they are at their best. They see that data and feelings both count. This balanced view can apply to everyday tasks, bigger life decisions, or even moral questions about right and wrong.

Advice for Non-Libras

If you are not a Libra, you can still use these ideas. Maybe you notice you jump to conclusions or speak harshly in arguments. Trying out Libra's calmer style might improve your relationships. Or if you rarely think about whether each voice is heard, you could practice letting quieter people speak in group chats.

None of this requires changing who you are. It simply means adopting better habits. If your sign is known for directness, adding a dash of Libra courtesy can keep dialogues smooth. If your sign is known for being shy, you can still adopt Libra's knack for fairness by ensuring your opinions do not get lost.

The Ongoing Need for Polite Diplomacy

In a busy world with many contrasting opinions, polite diplomacy remains crucial. Political debates, social media arguments, or even family discussions often get heated. People might forget to treat each other with respect. Libra's approach can reduce some of this tension.

That does not mean "avoid tough subjects." It means handle them with understanding. A Libra viewpoint says you can address complex issues—like how to distribute resources or how to handle disagreements—without insults or ignoring one side. If enough people adopt that approach, we might solve more problems peacefully.

Learning from the Other Signs

While Libra has many gifts, it also benefits from traits of the other signs. For example, from Aries, Libra can learn decisive action. From Taurus, it can learn patience and steadiness. From Cancer, it can learn deeper empathy. From Virgo, thorough planning. From Scorpio, emotional courage. From Sagittarius, optimism. From Capricorn, discipline. From Aquarius, innovative ideas. From Pisces, compassion. From Leo, self-confidence. From Gemini, quick thinking.

This cross-learning means that no sign stands alone. Each has strong points that can improve Libra's style. If a Libra recognizes they are stuck in overthinking, they might adopt a bit of Aries's boldness. Or if they are ignoring deeper issues, they might recall Scorpio's skill at going below the surface. This synergy is the beauty of the zodiac's variety.

Revisiting Common Misconceptions

Some people say Libras are only about looks or can never decide. We learned these are exaggerations. Yes, Libras care about appearances, but that is not all they care about. Yes, they weigh options, but they can and do make decisions. By seeing the deeper side of Libra—moral fairness, gentle strength—we realize it is more than surface-level politeness.

If you identify as Libra, remembering this can boost your confidence. You are not "indecisive forever." You simply make sure you gather enough facts. And your desire for peace is not "weakness." It often requires patience and courage to hold people together when tempers flare.

Personal Growth Strategies

For a Libra wanting to grow, consider these tips:

Set Boundaries: Practice respectfully telling others "I can't right now" or "I need time to think."

Make Timely Choices: If you realize you are stuck in endless pros and cons, pick a date or time to finalize your decision.

Speak Up: If something bothers you, address it politely but firmly before it becomes a bigger issue.

Balance Logic and Emotion: Check facts and consider feelings. This ensures solutions truly work for everyone.

Why Libra's Approach Endures

The symbol of the scales has survived thousands of years, featured in myths and legal emblems. People keep returning to the idea that a balanced outcome is a worthy goal. Even in a fast-paced, competitive age, we crave fairness. That is why Libra's approach, though sometimes gentle, remains powerful. It is a reminder that we are social beings, not just single-minded achievers.

In business or personal matters, success often hinges on fair dealings. Customers come back to honest merchants. Friends stay loyal when you treat them kindly. Even in creative fields, a well-balanced design or storyline captures attention. Libra's approach taps into these realities, making it relevant across time and cultures.

Embodying Libra Values Daily

Maybe the simplest way to sum up Libra's lesson is: strive for balance. This can mean balancing work and rest, alone time and social time, or seriousness and fun. It can mean giving your side in an argument but hearing the other side too. It might even mean balancing your budget, ensuring you do not overspend.

Each small act of balance can improve life. If you notice yourself leaning too far in one direction—like focusing only on your own ambitions or ignoring your own needs while helping others—pull back. Let the scales move to the middle. Doing so regularly can become a habit, leading to healthier, happier relationships.

Reflections on Libra's Symbol

If you imagine actual scales, each side can hold weight. If one side is too heavy, it dips. The device only works if you keep adjusting until both sides are level. Think of daily events as weights on each side: tasks, emotions, demands from others, personal goals. Each day, you might shift something from one side to the other—maybe you delegate a chore, say no to an extra project, or spend some time resting.

Over time, you develop an instinct for noticing imbalance earlier. That is the Libra method: do not wait for a meltdown or a giant conflict. Keep adjusting the small details so that harmony remains. This flexible, ongoing approach is more realistic than setting a strict routine and never changing. Real life shifts constantly, so your sense of balance must move with it.

Looking Back at Libra's Ancient Roots

The zodiac symbol for Libra, an object rather than an animal or mythical creature, shows that the sign focuses on a concept rather than raw energy. Ancient star-watchers saw a shape in the sky that suggested scales. They tied it to fairness, justice, and shared agreements. These ideas shaped laws, commerce, and moral lessons in many cultures, as we have seen.

Even if we do not read star maps the same way today, the underlying message remains: there is value in measuring, in checking each side, in being sure nothing is unfairly weighted. That practical wisdom guided farmers selling crops, judges in court, or even children sharing sweets.

Planetary Ruler: Venus

Libra's link to Venus suggests love, beauty, and social warmth. Libra tends to apply these to partnerships: building pleasing bonds, fostering respectful dialogues, and creating nice settings for interactions. This can be romantic love, friendship, teamwork, or community ties. In each case, the Libra approach is to keep things gentle yet honest.

While many signs express love differently, Libra's style is notably graceful. They might show affection by maintaining a pleasant tone, doing considerate acts, or giving gifts with an eye for detail. It might not be the most fiery or dramatic expression, but it can be deeply caring in its own consistent way.

Trust and Reliability

People often trust Libras, viewing them as neutral parties who will not cheat or judge unfairly. Of course, any individual can break trust, but Libra's typical nature leans toward being a fair partner or friend. This can be a big advantage in personal or career relationships. If you are seen as impartial and kind, people are more willing to confide in you.

Libras should guard that trust by avoiding favoritism. If you are the mediator in a dispute, keep your mind open. If you have a personal stake, be clear about it so no one feels misled. Transparency upholds that Libra reputation for fairness.

Advice for Everyday Libra Living

Whether you are a Libra or simply want to adopt these principles, a few practical steps include:

Morning Mindset: Each morning, think about tasks you must do. Decide how you will share or plan them fairly with co-workers, family, or friends.

Midday Check: After lunch, quickly reflect on your day. Are you leaning too heavily on one side (work, socializing, or chores)? If so, adjust.

Evening Reflection: Before sleeping, ask if you handled your interactions politely. Did you address conflicts in a balanced way or push them aside? If you see improvement, note it. If not, think about how to do better next time.

Setting Up Space: Arrange your room or workspace in a tidy, pleasant way that relaxes you and helps you welcome others. Even small touches, like a neat desk or a simple piece of artwork, can lift the mood.

Continued Learning

The lessons of Libra do not stop once you feel "fair enough." Each new challenge—be it a major conflict or a small decision—tests whether you can stay calm, weigh sides, and keep respectful boundaries. Life changes as you grow older, face new jobs, or move to new places, requiring you to adapt your balancing skills.

There is always more to learn. You might find better ways to phrase disagreements without sounding soft. You might find new methods to share tasks. The more you practice, the more natural it becomes. Over time, you might become the person others seek when tensions rise, knowing you can keep a cool head.

The Broader Impact

Imagine if entire communities decided to weigh each other's views more fairly, or if leaders consistently listened to all sides. Problems would still appear, but perhaps the path to solutions would be calmer. On a smaller scale, each of us can do our part by being kinder in daily chats, not forcing our opinions, and giving credit where due. That is how Libra's influence can ripple outward, from personal life to society at large.

Even in small ways—like letting someone go ahead in line or not hogging conversation—these acts of courtesy contribute to a friendlier environment. Many of these gestures cost nothing but show respect. Over time, they shape a group's culture, turning interactions from tense to supportive.

Final Reflections

Libra's symbol, the scales, continues to speak to us because balance is something we all seek, whether in emotions, relationships, or society. By exploring Libra's traits—its push for fairness, gentle communication, empathy, and harmony—we see that these values matter everywhere. They are found in law courts, family dinners, business meetings, and community gatherings. They help hold everything together, preventing one side from dominating.

As we conclude this book, remember that Libra is more than just a zodiac sign. It is a reminder to pause and check if things are even, if everyone is heard, if kindness is present. In a fast-changing world, those who keep a balanced perspective can guide others toward understanding. Whether you consider yourself a Libra or not, applying these ideas can add calm and fairness to the spaces you share with others. That is the heart of Libra's teaching: measure carefully, stand for equality, and nurture respectful connections wherever you go.

Help Us Share Your Thoughts!

Dear reader,

Thank you for spending your time with this book. We hope it brought you enjoyment and a few new ideas to think about. If there was anything that didn't work for you, or if you have suggestions on how we can improve, please let us know at **kontakt@skriuwer.com**. Your feedback means a lot to us and helps us make our books even better.

If you enjoyed this book, we would be very grateful if you left a review on the site where you purchased it. Your review not only helps other readers find our books, but also encourages us to keep creating more stories and materials that you'll love.

By choosing Skriuwer, you're also supporting **Frisian**—a minority language mainly spoken in the northern Netherlands. Although **Frisian** has a rich history, the number of speakers is shrinking, and it's at risk of dying out. Your purchase helps fund resources to preserve and promote this language, such as educational programs and learning tools. If you'd like to learn more about Frisian or even start learning it yourself, please visit **www.learnfrisian.com**.

Thank you for being part of our community. We look forward to sharing more books with you in the future.

Warm regards,
The Skriuwer Team

www.ingramcontent.com/pod-product-compliance
Lightning Source LLC
LaVergne TN
LVHW012040070526
838202LV00056B/5549